P9-CCB-832

Go Beyond the Job Description

Go Beyond the Job Description

A Complete Guide to Optimizing Talents, Skills, and Strengths in Organizations

Ashley Prisant Lesko, SHRM-CP

Society for Human Resource Management
Alexandria, Virginia
www.shrm.org

Strategic Human Resource Management India
Mumbai, India
www.shrmindia.org

Society for Human Resource Management
Haidian District Beijing, China
www.shrm.org/cn

Society for Human Resource Management, Middle East and Africa Office
Dubai, UAE
www.shrm.org/pages/mena.aspx

SOCIETY FOR HUMAN
RESOURCE MANAGEMENT

Copyright © 2018 Ashley Prisant Lesko. All rights reserved.

This publication is designed to provide accurate and authoritative information regarding the subject matter covered. It is sold with the understanding that neither the publisher nor the author is engaged in rendering legal or other professional service. If legal advice or other expert assistance is required, the services of a competent, licensed professional should be sought. The federal and state laws discussed in this book are subject to frequent revision and interpretation by amendments or judicial revisions that may significantly affect employer or employee rights and obligations. Readers are encouraged to seek legal counsel regarding specific policies and practices in their organizations.

This book is published by the Society for Human Resource Management (SHRM). The interpretations, conclusions, and recommendations in this book are those of the author and do not necessarily represent those of the publisher.

This publication may not be reproduced, stored in a retrieval system, or transmitted in whole or in part, in any form or by any means, electronic, mechanical, photocopying, recording, or otherwise, without the prior written permission of the publisher, or authorization through payment of the appropriate per-copy fee to the Copyright Clearance Center, Inc., 222 Rosewood Drive, Danvers, MA 01923, 978-750-8600, fax 978-646-8600, or on the Web at www.copyright.com. Requests to the publisher for permission should be addressed to SHRM Book Permissions, 1800 Duke Street, Alexandria, VA 22314, or online at http://www.shrm.org/about-shrm/pages/copyright--permissions.aspx. SHRM books and products are available on most online bookstores and through the SHRMStore at www.shrmstore.org.

The Society for Human Resource Management is the world's largest HR professional society, representing 285,000 members in more than 165 countries. For nearly seven decades, the Society has been the leading provider of resources serving the needs of HR professionals and advancing the practice of human resource management. SHRM has more than 575 affiliated chapter within the United States and subsidiary offices in China, India, and United Arab Emirates. Please visit us at www.shrm.org.

Library of Congress Cataloging-in-Publication Data has been applied for and is on file with the Library of Congress.

ISBN (pbk)   978-1-586-44517-1
ISBN (PDF)   978-1-586-44518-8
ISBN (EPUB)   978-1-586-44519-5
ISBN (MOBI)   978-1-586-44520-1

Printed in the United States of America

FIRST EDITION

PB Printing   10 9 8 7 6 5 4 3 2 1

61.xxxx| 18-000

This book is dedicated to all of those who know they are more than the job description says they are.

Table of Contents

Foreword

Going Beyond: Foundations, Mission, and Perspective

When Ashley Lesko first asked me to write the foreword for *Go Beyond the Job Description* I was surprised and excited for the opportunity. I'm excited to be a part of this great book because it can help leaders at every level. After I got over the surprise and excitement, I felt the weight of the responsibility to write something worthy of the words that would follow. I've done my best to provide an honest and compelling recommendation for this book for you, the person reading these words. You may be reading these words as the first step to reading the entire book or to determine if you should buy this book. If it is the latter, buy it. I'm confident you will enjoy reading it and, more importantly, you will benefit from reading it *if* you use the plan Ashley explains so well in the pages to follow.

My confidence in making a recommendation for *Go Beyond the Job Description* lies in the foundation of the book; using short stories to make a point or emphasize a concept is one of my favorite tools in my leadership toolbox. Learning through other people's experience is valuable. I have a friend and mentor who once told me it takes 20 years to get 20 years of experience; he's right, but a person can also gain insight and understanding through another person's experience. The degree to which that understanding occurs is mostly dependent on how well the experience is conveyed. Having said all that, Ashley does a great job of organizing and delivering the experiences of others. She provides a perspective on the experiences and enables the reader to understand principles and concepts in a context that matters. Facts without context are useless ... facts without the proper context are misleading; Ashley provides the context that allows the reader to gain the most from the experiences of others.

Another leadership tool I like is the checklist. I quickly realized the value of a checklist when I was a young sailor on a nuclear submarine; checklists are easy to use, provide clear direction to successfully accomplish something, and most importantly, if used properly, prevent mistakes. The checklist approach is the foundation of a plan Ashley lays out that is achievable because it is actionable. Too many people dream or talk about ideas but fail to *plan* to realize those dreams or execute those plans; this book provides the plan for leaders to allow their teams to go beyond their job descriptions and achieve more than they otherwise thought they could.

As a career Navy officer, my principal job is to lead others to achieve the mission of my organization. Leaders must play the hand they are dealt to achieve the goals of the organization. The best leaders know their people and leverage their people's talents to best support their mission. This book provides a framework to do exactly that—leverage the talents of your people to accomplish more with the same resources. One of the first definitions of a leader I learned is "a person who motivates others to achieve more, as a team, than they could ever have achieved as individuals." This book provides a plan to help motivate others to achieve more, to go beyond their job description and grow as individuals, all of which helps the organization.

I hope you enjoy reading this book and gain a perspective that can help your team realize their potential and help your organization achieve its goals.

—Sam Pennington, Captain, US Navy

Talent Engagement and Advancing Your Career Steps

I have had the privilege and pleasure of working with Dr. Lesko for many years, and I have always been struck by her keen ability to motivate and inspire others. She has a deep passion for talent and leadership development. More importantly, she is passionate about sharing her knowledge through her consulting practice and teaching at Harvard Extension School. This book is a great manifestation of her passion for sharing her knowledge, and I am very honored to write this introduction!

Firstly, this book has very insightful concepts that are relevant and prescient. Secondly, each concept is explained and demonstrated further with real-life stories and examples. Thirdly, it is written with a lot of heart in very easy-to-understand language so that anyone can learn and enjoy it. Finally, and most importantly, this book provides a practical 100-day playbook with clear steps to help you succeed utilizing a well-thought-out framework of what → who → how → when. I hope that you will enjoy this book and find it extremely useful, as I have. Happy reading!

—Ritesh Chaturbedi, Chief Strategy & Technology Officer, Preferred

The Power of Potential

We are all capable of achieving more. How much we achieve is often directly impacted by the people who surround us, no matter how much inner drive we have. Supportive friends and family can challenge us to stretch ourselves and provide a place to safely land and regroup when we fall short. Our colleagues and leadership at work can push us far beyond what we ever felt capable of, or push us completely out of our chosen career.

Leadership is a privilege that carries with it the responsibility to maximize the potential of everyone around us—especially when individuals don't see the potential in themselves. This requires an intentional, consistent effort to see beyond where someone has been, or where she is now, and project how far she can go. Not all leaders are capable of shouldering this responsibility, and some leaders don't even want to be bothered with it.

As a certified forensic interviewer, I've realized that the best interviewers and the best leaders share the same two core skills: vision and influence. They can visualize a future state that others are unable to, and they have the ability to influence people to commit to achieving that state, even in the face of obstacles. Great interviewers don't say to themselves "He is just a criminal" or "She couldn't have seen anything important where she was standing" or "He was at a drug deal, so I can't believe what he says." Great interviewers go into every interview with an open mind and a learning mentality that allows them to gather as much information as possible and positions them to verify what they learn after the interview. Great leaders don't say to themselves "That's all he's ever done, so that's all he can do" or "She went to school for something different, so she won't fit" or "He comes from a different industry, so he could never understand." Great leaders look at everyone and what they've done previously and ask themselves "How can this person make me better, and how far can we go together?"

It was a leader with this mindset who gave me my first career break. I had been working for a retail store for about 18 months when my district manager, Adam, approached me about interviewing for a manager's position. It was a bit of a surprise as I had started as a seasonal employee on the loading dock, transitioned to a part-time loss prevention position, went back to the loading dock full time, and then transitioned back into loss prevention full time, spending about six months in each role. I was a little more surprised when I learned that the open manager's position was in a regional pilot store with significant inventory-control issues. This meant that the store was a high-visibility location that received many visits from corporate leadership and had significant operations and theft issues that needed to be corrected.

I agreed to take the interview, and several weeks later Adam drove me three and a half hours to what would soon become my new store. In the car, Adam was honest and told me that I was one of four candidates, that I had the least experience, and that one of the candidates had previously worked in this store. During the interview I knew I couldn't focus on my previous experience, so I focused on the future of the store and what we could do together. Two days later I was officially offered the job and unknowingly took the first steps toward what would become my career. With Adam's support and motivation, we made such significant progress that I was transferred to the company's largest store in the continental United States 364 days after I accepted the job.

Flashing forward several years, I had moved on to another retailer and continued to find success. Once again, I was presented with an unexpected opportunity. I was granted the chance to interview for what I felt would be a career-defining opportunity. Once again, I was one of four candidates, and I had the least amount of experience. I flew out to Chicago for the interview and thankfully did well enough that I was offered the job at the conclusion of the interview. Several months later I was finally told the truth about how I was perceived before the interview. Coming into my interview I was openly referred to as "pig bait," meaning that I was brought in to make the other candidates look better. Thankfully my new team was aware enough to see past their preconceptions, to identify potential, and to choose the candidate they thought offered them the brightest future.

These are just two of dozens of examples of people who believed that what I could become was far beyond what I had been. There were plenty of times in my career when I didn't believe in my own potential. If it weren't for this small army of supporters, who knows where I would be today. I almost certainly wouldn't have had the opportunity to partner with Ashley.

Ashley and I weren't aware of our respective backgrounds when we were first introduced. However, after one short conversation, we felt we had enough in common to schedule a follow-up meeting and explore the opportunities that we might be able to create together. During that first meeting, we discovered our shared passion for looking beyond what a person's résumé says and focusing on his or her potential. It has been a pleasure to work with Ashley and to recommend her to colleagues ever since.

Truly unique perspectives can be very hard to find today. Ashley's military, corporate, academic, and entrepreneurial experience galvanize to form a perspective that can't be shared by many other leaders. She has been through so many diverse challenges, with so many diverse teams, which have taught her how to identify talent and motivate people to achieve their best. Combine her experience and perspective with her love for her teams, and you have a truly unique and valuable resource.

As you read this book, you will undoubtedly relate it to your world, your experience, and your teams. You will be inspired to try new approaches, and you will likely look back and think about how you could've handled things differently. As you look back on your prior experiences, please don't think of any of them as mistakes. You made the best decision you could at those times with the tools you had available. Now that you are integrating new leadership tools, you can learn from your previous experiences and improve how you handle similar future events.

I will never forget what Adam told me after I was hired for that first manager's position. He looked at me, smiled, and said "I always believed that if you wait until someone is ready to promote them, then it's already too late." As you read through Ashley's experience and strategies, please remember you have the opportunity to shape the lives and careers of everyone you work with. You can choose to rely on a résumé or what someone's past experience appears to tell you about them. Or you can take the time to connect with them, learn about who they are as a person, and open their eyes to potential they may not even realize they have. Most leaders choose not to take this path. Hopefully you will.

—*Michael Reddington, CFI, VP of Executive Education,*
Wicklander-Zulawski and Associates

Acknowledgments

This book has been a long time coming—both personally and professionally. I have peppered the book with personal stories of the reasons why I felt that I needed to go beyond the job description; some places I was able to do so, and other times that I learned I was not allowed.

Professionally, this book is in line to help leaders bring their teams into the 2nd quarter of the 21st century. We take none of the words our own leaders say for granted—instead, we just look it up on the Internet to see if it's fact. We look at information differently than we did 50, 25, even 10 years ago. As a result, we look at our employees and our leaders differently because the information is not black and white any more, can come from so many sources, and has so many shades of gray.

I want to first thank my family. To my mom who taught me how to lead in the face of adversity—thank you. My children, Jonathan and Sydney, who are a source of energy, and sometimes even a bit of guidance. (Who knew?) To the rest of my family who have listened to my ideas for years (you know who you are)... thank you (and I promise more are coming!).

The stories in Part 4 of each chapter are true and based on experiences of people in many industries, education levels, experiences, leaderships styles, and more. I want to thank each of them for their willingness to share their experiences and opening their own viewpoints so that you could benefit. Special thanks to Michael Reddington, Sam Pennington, and Ritesh Chaturbedi for going above and beyond at every level.

I want to thank Raakin Hossain, my first "editor" and the one that gave encouragement from the beginning—ideas when they stopped showing up—and some caulk for the holes I sometimes created. You are your own Mr. Penumbra, and your story is only the beginning.

To the individuals that know you're more than your job description—don't ever let anyone tell you otherwise. It took me many years to realize I went beyond every day—and further than many people could appreciate. Don't let others' viewpoints on your job or your contribution slow you down. Find ways every day to go beyond—for yourself.

To my readers—thank you for making this possible. I look forward to hearing your stories (visit squarepegsolutions.org to share your story) as to how you went beyond the job description and even how you made TEO (talent-engagement optimization) successful in your organization.

Why You Picked Up This Book (and How to Use It Now That You Have It)

Introduction

Getting Started

Each chapter in this book will start with a short story about a company called Smoky Bay Sporting Goods (SBSG), a company on the cusp of something great—developing a talent-engagement program and helping its people go beyond their job descriptions. In this section, we talk about the reasons why you also want to start a talent-engagement program, how to do it, and what reasons would cause you to go down this path.

For me, it started with good intentions. I took an assessment and learned that, well, I was a teacher and a learner. I probably already knew this to some extent, but it took this assessment that clarified it in writing to make it real.

The only problem was that I was not teaching, or learning (much). I was in operations at the time and didn't have the chance to create new learning or understanding really for anyone. I went to my manager and told him what I wanted to do (teach) and asked if there was a way I could give back to our team or organization.

There was.

At the time, leadership-development training in our company was in transition, and as a result, numerous teams were left wanting for a better direction to point their leaders. He asked me if I could develop some training sessions—something to help bridge the gap.

I did, willingly, and loved it.

My manager learned my strengths and allowed me to *go beyond my job description.* I was still required to complete my normal job functions, which I did, but I had a new source of motivation—one that had me doing my own job better, faster, and more efficiently while helping his team, the department, and the organization as a whole by doing something I enjoyed. The team got better. I got better. It was a win-win. And we never spent a dollar for it.

This is the story of how you can do that. Go beyond the job description.

The Nuts and Bolts

What Is Talent Engagement?

I always hate when a book jumps in without starting with the basics—that is, what we're actually doing here. Let's start at the beginning with a definition. What is talent engagement?

Talent engagement is maximizing your employees' output to the team, department, and organization by using both the stated requirements for the job and the talents, skills, and strengths not listed in the job description.

Maximizing talent engagement requires the following:

- Each employee knows his or her own strengths and talents.
- Each leadership team knows employee strengths and talents.
- Each employee uses his or her strengths and talents at work.

Another way to maximize talent engagement is to optimize it—to use as much as possible of the talent the employee is willing to engage.

Your *talent-engagement optimization (TEO)* project will be just that: your action plan on optimizing the talent in your company—the employees you already have—and creating a more motivated, efficient, and energized workforce that works around silos and sees beyond the basics of what is required of it.

Why Develop Talent Engagement?

There are 168 hours in a week, and with any luck, you're only working 40–50 of those. Within those hours, however, are a million different tasks, requirements, and needs that you and everyone else around you are trying to complete. Why should you develop your talent engagement? What about the talent engagement in others?

DO YOU HAVE AN UNSEEN PICASSO?

Stop for a second. What do you do really well? What is the skill or strength that, if you could use it for the majority of your job, you would just rock it out—really enjoy the job or do it well? Are you a builder of relationships? A salesperson or competitor to the nth degree? A developer of others? I'm not looking at your job title; I'm looking at skill sets, soft skills, and talents.

We all have talents. We each have a combination of talents or skills that no one else has. It's due to your life experiences, your training, your personality—or maybe a combination. No one has lived your life. You could have "real" or tangible talents—an amazing singing voice, a facility with numbers—or those that are harder to see, such as being a stellar motivator, leader, or learner.

What talents or strengths do you have right now that you're not using? Do you have a talent that is hidden and that you would like to be using? Is there a way you could use it every day? Could you find a way?

A few years ago, I decided to go back to school (again) to get my PhD. It wasn't the easiest thing and I changed my life once again, balancing a full-time job, family, kids, and school. But teaching others helped me realize that I not only liked to teach, I *loved* it. It was my unseen Picasso.

To help others learn a topic or see a concept in a different light based on their own experiences was an *amazing experience* for me. However, I was not in a training or teaching position and didn't have the opportunity at the time to change over. I talked to my manager about a way to teach his department, and he agreed—I would train his employees over the course of several months in a short leadership-development program to help them learn more about themselves and others.

It was a great experience for all involved. I got to embrace my unseen Picasso—something I had a talent for and worked on in my own time if needed—which motivated me in my regular job as well. The department staff members got to benefit from training and talent development when they would have had none. My manager took a chance on me, and I appreciate to this day what his trust in me did for my motivation at the time.

So, I bring it back to you. You may have to take a chance. For yourself, for your team, or maybe even both. What is your unseen Picasso? Feel free to jot down your thoughts here. What would you like to do more of at work that you don't do now?

_____

_____

_____

_____

_____

In the upcoming chapters, I will ask you the questions again: What is your unseen Picasso? Where is the talent engagement in others? I challenge you to think about what you would like to do on your job—if you could—that would benefit the company. What if everyone on your team did that? What if everyone in the company did it?

Increasing talent engagement will help increase motivation, efficiency, and initiative in individuals—in you, your team, and even your boss. Oh, and if it's done right, it can be done with little to no money.

You already have the talent. How can you leverage the time and energy that the individuals are already putting in?

TALENT ENGAGEMENT VERSUS EMPLOYEE ENGAGEMENT

For those of you who come from the HR world or for leaders who have worked with a company that has jumped on the employee engagement (EE) train, you can probably give examples—in great detail—of what employee engagement is. (You can probably do it better than I can!) Simply defined, EE is the attitude of a person about a job (Rothwell 2010). EE can be broken out by employee characteristics such as job satisfaction, motivation (internally, for success and job accomplishment), and work commitment (Chat-Uthai 2013).

You may sometimes hear *workplace engagement* used interchangeably for EE. Workplace engagement is defined as reducing burnout at work by increasing three areas for employees: the vigor in an employee's efforts, dedication of an employee to his or her job, and absorption of the employee with the job (Schaufeli and Baaker 2003). You can think of absorption as when you are deeply immersed in a task, and you take a few hours before taking a break—maybe even missing lunch!

Regardless of the term you use, both workplace engagement and employee engagement focus on getting individuals more engaged at work. Talent engagement, on the other hand, focuses on engaging the employee's *talents* and strengths at work. It is a more focused, targeted strategy to increase a specific area of an employee's contribution—resulting in an increase in employee engagement *and* in company productivity and objectives being met.

Purpose of This Book

I've been there: You need a quick bang for your buck, or your leadership team members won't buy in to your solution. You need to say it in the right way or convince them of a certain idea before anything moves forward. Oh, and you have to have the budget for any of it to start.

I had this challenge. I didn't have the budget, and at different times, I wasn't senior enough to get the footing (or support) I needed for the leadership team to listen to the changes I proposed.

Other companies I've worked with have faced this challenge too. They recognized the need but couldn't balance the budget with additional support from the outside for trainers, consultants, and more.

I got tired of hitting brick walls, so I decided to climb over them. This book is *a 100-day action plan* to building talent engagement for your team, department, or organization. If you follow the chapters in this book—created as a checklist—then your team will be *10–15 percent more effective in its work,* that is, the team members will do 10–15 percent more in their day than they used to.

That result could mean 10–15 percent more projects, training, or areas you haven't even thought of yet (but they have).

This book is an action plan—*your* action plan. You will be the leader of the plan, and to be successful, you will need to be engaged and willing to open yourself up to new opportunities (you've already read this far, so you're halfway there!).

It's your action plan. You, your team, and your organization *must* put your touch, your culture, and your flavor on it. I am a believer that theory is nothing without examples, and this book is full of them. Each company and team is different, so I encourage you to modify the plan to what works for you. If you find a new way, I encourage you to then tell us about it—you may be able to help someone else in the future!

Who This Book Is Written For

This book is written for people who want to make an impact but don't have a lot of room, time, or money to do so:

- *Leaders of teams ranging from two to fifty* who know their team has more talent and time but are unsure of ways to tap into it, who want to rein in the hiring process, who need to reduce spending and expenses, and who know they want to help their teams get the most out of what they already have.
- *HR and operations consultants.* Yes, both groups can benefit from this book. The HR consultants will learn about the operations (behind the scenes) that will help them track metrics and quantify the processes. The operations consultants will learn the people aspect that puts qualitative data into perspective.
- *HR managers and directors for small to midsize companies* who want to make a culture impact and increase initiatives in their organizations.

- *Training managers for midsize to large companies* who want to change the way their teams are looking at training and finding ways to benefit from useful employee skills that are not always obvious for an organization.
- *Individual contributors* who want to understand how to create a more efficient workflow and process. They can also find out how to increase their own talent engagement—leading to a more rewarding workplace.

Why You Should Use This Book

I did some research a while ago about why people leave companies (Lesko 2016b). Why should you use it? Simply put, to get more out of your people so that they feel like a valued part of your group and company and, ultimately, so that your good employees don't leave.

I Didn't Quit My Job, I Fired My Company

Have you ever quit a job? If so, why? When I asked this question in the pilot study, one of the key statistics that stuck out was that 92 percent of people said they quit because of management.

Think about it. It wasn't the benefits, the salary, or even the co-workers. The top reason that people quit was because of the management team. What's even scarier than that? Sixty percent said that they quit because of their immediate manager.

You can counter this trend by knowing who you are and who your people are. This may sound a bit wishy-washy, but it's not. Nearly 40 percent of the survey respondents said that the environment or the culture of the firm led them to resign.

You hire people for a job description: accountant, buyer, sales representative, IT production support manager. You may even have several employees in each position. Yet each one of them is different. They have their own talents and their own strengths—including ones that are outside of their job description, but that align with *the company's strategic goals and values*. Finding out what their strengths and talents are and using them to the company's (and their own) advantage is called talent engagement, and it is a very powerful tool that helps you as a manager and leader of your company get more out of your employees by giving them more.

You also invest in them as individuals. They are learning new skills on the job and using them to help the organization achieve its overall business goals How can you further invest in their human capital? How can you make the organization a better workplace for them? At the end of the day, you want to retain the talent that you helped grow.

Most of the time, people do not look forward to quitting their jobs or firing their companies. They are looking for reasons to stay. Increasing talent engagement is a way to help them do that.

Give them a way to give more.

How to Use This Workbook

In the words of Po in the movie *Kung Fu Panda*, "enough chit-chat." Let's get started. There are five sections and twelve chapters in this book:

- Section 1. How to Use This Book (*you are here*)
- Section 2. The First 25 Days—Chapters 1–3
- Section 3. Days 26–50—Chapters 4–6
- Section 4. Days 51–75—Chapters 7–9
- Section 5. The Last 25 Days—Chapters 10–12

Each chapter contains four parts:

- **Part 1. The SBSG Story.** Each chapter has a short story about Smoky Bay Sporting Goods (SBSG), a continuing anecdote that follows Elizabeth and her team as they implement TEO in their organization. The challenges, solutions, and results that she and her team face tend to be very similar to those that other organizations may find when implementing TEO.
- **Part 2. The Nuts and Bolts.** You'll find the heavy hitters of the chapter in this area: concepts to explain the theories, research to support the reasoning, and additional knowledge or background. If you want to quickly understand the goals and purpose of the chapter, start here.
- **Part 3. Activities and Application.** Start here if you want to learn *how* to achieve the concepts in the chapter. This part is set up like a workbook, and you will actually apply what you've learned in the previous parts of the chapter and build the action plan, think through questions, or assess your project at the given time.
- **Part 4. Real Stories.** It's one thing for me to say it, but it's entirely another thing to hear it from other people. These stories come from all industries and settings—corporate, government, and military field and office. They come from all organizational and experience levels. Listen to the stories of people who have been there—who have struggled, failed, and succeeded.

I spent several years in the military, and it created a love of checklists I still have today. The book is written in timeline and checklist fashion. If you want to complete your TEO project with all the steps, then I would suggest reading through the chapters, building your own rough timeline, and then working through the book with your team members in tow (don't read the book to them—just lead them through your action plan!).

There are a few stops along the way—chapters that help you secure buy-in with individuals or that share ways to prevent (or deal with) roadblocks in your project. They have been placed in the timeline where I and other professionals have most frequently seen them, but you may want to jump ahead (or go back) as needed.

The book is to be used at your discretion. However, you are bound to find useful tips and tricks of the trade throughout as it combines tried-and-true strategies from the HR, operations, and project management fields. You might already know a lot of this information from your work experience, but I believe you will also find ways to use it to articulate your business plan to others or even understand it better yourself by reading it from this perspective.

The Best Way to Succeed with This Book—Guidelines for Actually Completing This Project

Step 1. Get leadership buy-in. It's the place I've probably failed the most—communicating clearly enough to get my senior leaders to actually do what I'm asking them to do for the organization. Actions are greater than words, and you'll need a bit of both to get this accomplished. Leaders need to know what's in it for them, what the project is going to cost, and a few more details. Start with Chapter 1 to help complete this step for greatest success!

Step 2. Get team buy-in. The team is the group of individuals—and their leaders— who will most feel the effects of your TEO project. Collaborate as much as possible. Chapter 2 talks about securing the team's support in terms of the change they will feel, and Chapter 6 deals with their viewpoints to help you steer them in the right direction.

Step 3. Know what it costs. The TEO project is not very expensive in terms of dollars, but it can take time, and it is an investment in talents and efforts. Chapters 1, 3, and 5 address different costs of the project, and a few that may be hidden (such as leaders who are not involved in the project but want to know the results— leading to extra time spent for both you and the leader!).

Step 4. Know what success looks like (which metrics to measure by). Chapter 1 explores this area. TEO focuses on areas such as increased *talent engagement, productivity, efficiency* (doing more in less time), *initiative, happiness,* and *employee engagement* (although different from talent engagement, employee engagement is still an area that can be positively affected). What do you want to improve?

Other metrics could be a reduction in labor hours or elimination of a future need to hire employees (due to efficiency gains). Select the metrics that you want to focus on and how you will measure them. Chapter 11 addresses this along with benchmarking—it can be a survey, a before-and-after interview, a measurement of work, or an assessment.

Don't forget to measure before implementing the TEO project—using the Talent Engagement Zone survey, for example, or one of your own. There are scales and assessments for each.

Suggested metrics for your TEO project include the following:

- *Talent engagement.* Talent Engagement Zone, dirty work assessment.
- *Productivity.* Hours used for a task before versus after, labor plan comparison, interview questionnaire.
- *Efficiency.* Number of hours needed to complete a process, number of hours allocated to other areas such as training.
- *Initiative.* Initiative scale comparison (before and after), interview questionnaire.
- *Happiness.* Happiness at work assessment.
- *Employee engagement.* The Utrecht Work Engagement Scale (UWES) (see Chapter 3) or other engagement surveys.

You're Not Alone

You have started walking down an interesting path—one that can help your company by just giving it what you already have. Tap into those strengths, and flex your muscles. The ride begins today.

SECTION 2

The First 25 Days (Finding the "What")

CHAPTER 1

Get on the Train: Leaving the Station with More Than What You Had When You Started Out

1.1 The SBSG Story

Joe stands up slowly from his desk, removing his reading glasses from the bridge of his nose. It's nearly time to meet with Tyler, the CEO of SBSG and Joe's boss and long-time friend. Friend, yes, but not without their challenges. Joe is the VP of operations for the company and has been there for five years. With 50 stores in the tristate area, SBSG is trying to figure out how to grow profits without spending more on employee expenses. It hasn't been easy.

He looks up to see Elizabeth knocking on his open door. "Ready, boss?"

He nods. Elizabeth has been with the company for three years and is making headway in leaps and bounds. She is the operations manager for the main fulfillment center for the stores, at least in title. In actuality, she has tried to do much more—from operations, to customer service (where she started with the company and worked for about eight months), to finance (although no one, he thinks, would give her the accounting books any time soon!).

Joe and Elizabeth are going to talk to Tyler about a new concept—talent engagement optimization—that Elizabeth wants to implement within SBSG to help employees go beyond their own job description while contributing more to the company. At a minimum, she wants to lead her own department (HR), but if she gets some interest from other department leaders as "early adopters," perhaps also operations, accounting, and marketing to the project.

Joe thinks it sounds a bit too good to be true, but he has kept his thoughts to himself and agreed to let Elizabeth talk to Tyler about it. He presented it to Tyler as a developmental opportunity for Elizabeth.

Joe has to admit, Elizabeth did her due diligence. She had prepped for the questions that she thought Tyler would ask—as well as others that he doesn't ask. In the 30-minute meeting, Tyler is direct, as he always is. Working only from her notes, Elizabeth had prepared no presentation slides because she knows that Tyler's nature is neither to require nor request them.

After Elizabeth completes the basics of her points, Joe turns to her and nods. Nervously, she launches into her request. Tyler looks at her intensely, asking only occasional questions about the resources requested. She is prepared for some of his questions—but not all of them.

1.2 The Nuts and Bolts

Why are you here? If you read (or at least skimmed) through Section 1, you may have a few ideas based on what I suggested. If you skipped the section, you may want to review it when you get a chance.

Are you here because you want to help your team members or other employees in your organization get more out of their day? Their job? Their career path?

Are you here because you don't have a lot of money to spend on a large-scale transformational consulting project—but you need to make a change?

Are you here simply because you know the status quo just isn't cutting it, and you know that you can make your team better—but may need an outline or framework to do so?

Or something else?

The bottom line: You're here to help someone go beyond the job description. Whether it's a group of two employees, a team, or an entire organization, you believe there's a way to optimize each employee's talent engagement. We call this *talent engagement optimization (TEO)*—which is a mouthful to say that you are more than just a job—and this book will help you get more out of your team.

First, you need some support.

Getting Executive Buy-In

This is the first of several times you will see this as a header for your to-do list. If you are not at the top of the food chain in your organization (and 95 percent of us are not), you will have to find and convince the people at the top that your TEO project is worth pursuing. You may simply need their support—or you may also need their time, ongoing support (stated in an e-mail or in person to others), and resources (people, places, or money). At the very least, you will need their stamp of approval.

WHERE DO YOU START?

You will find I am a checklist person. Measuring your work is a great way to see that you've accomplished what you set out to do or are making progress. It's also one of three ways to prevent your job from becoming a "miserable job" (Lencioni 2007). Review the following list to help you cover your "executive buy-in" bases:

1. *Take a look at Part 1.3 and answer the first three questions.* These questions ask where you currently stand and where you want to go. Part 1.3 also contains a table allowing you to perform a gap analysis. This information is what you need to focus on, and you will build your action plan around it. Check out Section 1 on the best way to succeed with this book or Chapter 3 on how to assess to help you decide what areas you are going to measure.

2. *Build your goals.* Figure out where you'd like to be. Think about how long reaching your goals should take. The focus of this book is built around a 100-day action plan. You will not change the mindset of everyone in a 10,000-person company in that amount of time—but you could impact a department of 50 people who are looking for a transition (if they just don't know how to do it).

3. *Define success.* Yes, you've picked your goals, but what would success look like? If you were able to meet 50 percent of your goals within 100 days (or the time you choose)—is that success?

4. *Prepare your goals for your executive team.* The leader (or leaders) has a lot on their plate. What is important to them? What are the goals for the leader or the organization this year? How can you align your goals for this project with their goals?

5. *Brief your executive team.* At this point, you know what's best. It could be a quick e-mail saying "Hey, I'm doing this. Let me know if you have any issues. Otherwise, I'll let you know when I need your support." Or it could be a full presentation. Reference Section 1 or Chapter 11 (how to sell it and present it for results) for more information on best practices to do this.

6. *Define a flexible and tentative timeline* so the executive team knows when to start expecting yields after approving your project.

The above checklist will help you find what you need and gather executive buy-in. Many projects fail from not first getting buy-in, dooming the rest of the project before it starts. Check out the next chapter, which explains some of the reasons why projects like this fail.

TEO PROJECT TEAM TYPES

This book focuses on you as a leader. You may not be the leader of the group that you are working in—you could be an HR director, a chief operations officer (COO), a project manager, a consultant, or a part-time analyst. But for purposes of this book, regardless of your title in the organization, you *are* a leader. A leader is someone who influences others, and you will definitely be doing that in your TEO project. You are part of the team that is leading the TEO project to help your employee group go beyond the job description. You are the point person to make it happen. This book is here to support you to make sure that you are successful.

As such, from here out, I will refer to you as the "leader" of this project.

Now, what kind of team will you be leading? There are several types:

• *In-place team.* This is a traditional team of 2–25 people who are in the same group or department. For the most part, they also work at the same location. They generally do the same work (e.g., product management), although they may have different ranks or titles. The work is homogenous, but their viewpoints toward the work are anything but. Your challenges may be differentiating them and getting them to sing their best tune (noting that some of them can't sing, so you'll have to be creative for a few).

- *Hybrid team.* This team is still fairly traditional, but with a twist or blend. You have people from different departments, throughout the organization, or in different locations. The challenge with this team is that neither the work nor the viewpoints are homogenous. This group offers a greater chance for a project champion—someone in the group (or a few people) who can support it (so you're not the only one).
- *Virtual team.* This group is in many locations. Employees can be from the same department or in a hybrid environment, but they are in enough locations that change as a whole will be difficult for them. However, being spread over many locations can be a good thing in that negative Nancys will not be able to become roadblocks as quickly (see Chapter 8), but you have to work harder at communication. Having a virtual team can expand the reach of your TEO project and increase its opportunities in the future.

The idea of creating your TEO team is to define a target audience large enough to reach statistical significance but small enough to experiment your proposal to prove its value. Table 1.1 summarizes the types of teams.

TABLE 1.1.   Types of Teams

	IN-PLACE TEAM	HYBRID TEAM	VIRTUAL TEAM
Number of people (approx.)	2–25	5–40	2–40
Location	All in one place	Mostly in one place	Almost all in different places
Benefits	Homogenous tasks, generally same backgrounds and experiences	Opportunity for group leaders and project champions to support TEO project	Reduction of negativity and roadblocks in group
Disadvantages	Could be seen as too similar, but have drastically different viewpoints	Different tasks, backgrounds, and experiences	Communication strategy, getting information across individuals

1.3 Activities and Application

Starting the Application: Getting Executive Buy-In

You'll have the chance to fill out your action plan and the checklists for your TEO program in upcoming chapters. The three questions below pertain to the project and goal and will help get your wheels turning as you move toward collecting and analyzing the data to successfully implement your project:

- What is the goal of the project? What do you want to have at the end of the project?
- Where are you now in terms of reaching your goal? For example, if your goal is that 75 percent of the team will start taking initiative, are you currently at 25 percent?
- Have you done a gap analysis? Compare the previous two questions. Table 1.2 is set up for you to use as a guide.

TABLE 1.2. Gap Analysis

ITEM	CURRENT STATE/BEFORE	GOAL/FUTURE STATE/AFTER	DIFFERENCES/GAPS
Example Engagement level of accountants for career growth	Individuals do not care about taking initiative and do not seem interested in moving up—both of which are needed for this company	1. Want at least 25% of accounting team to show interest in moving to next level (management) 2. Want at least 75% of team to show initiative and to be proactive about problems vs. reactive	1. Need to improve career progression interests 2. Need to increase initiative measures

Now that you know what your goals are, the following questions will help you focus on buy-in and your specific stakeholders:

1. Who are the key people/leadership/executives that you need to keep informed about this project?
2. Whose buy-in do you need for this project?
3. Whose buy-in would be nice for you to have for this project?
4. In your initial discussions or e-mails, you requested support, confirmation, or buy-in from the people in questions one and two. What did you ask them? Note when you sent it and the time they or you set for a requested response. What did they say?
5. Are there any follow-up steps or tasks? Write them here, then load them in your task or to-do list for action on the appropriate date.
6. How will you check in with the stakeholders and leaders? You will eventually put the information from above in the action plan. But for now, while the meeting or e-mail is still fresh in your head—write down your thoughts about how you will communicate with them.
7. Get confirmation from your project sponsor if you are able and add any comments here:

_____

_____

_____

_____

_____

_____

_____

_____

1.4 Real Stories

In each of the following chapters, Part 4 shares stories from individuals around the world related to the topics in the chapter. The stories are aimed to provide some context and to reinforce what you just read in the rest of the chapter, and to give you suggestions, ideas, and support

Signing up 20 Leaders One Step at a Time

For the retail industry, the e-commerce strategy affects many business units (BUs)—sometimes disproportionately. Because of those impacts, many large retailers will require a global change in e-commerce strategy to have buy-in and agreement from as many as 20–25 BU leaders.

In my case, the retailer's e-commerce channel had 35-plus different shipping offers and thresholds depending on the product type and price. It was extremely confusing for a customer who had multiple items in their cart. Also, feedback from customers was that the overall user experience was very complex. This directly resulted in a high number of abandoned carts, which in essence were lost sales for the company. To provide a great customer experience and drive sales higher, we needed to drastically simplify our customer experience and provide our customers one single shipping threshold. There were many steps in this phase—from agreeing on threshold values to managing lower margins.

This was an enormous undertaking and, together, first we put a cross-functional team with members from top 10 BUs (total team size = 12: 10 BUs + 1 e-commerce + 1 leader). The cross-functional team got the data first with a benchmark of what other competitors were doing and did several steps to demonstrate that all inputs and assumptions were factored in.

They conducted extensive reviews with every BU leadership team to ensure their input and feedback were taken under consideration. Based on the feedback, the team had to reassess their plans. The team also conducted hundreds of sample tests to confirm their ideas. This helped validate their results with actual results. Finally, as the leader of the project, I spent a significant amount of time throughout the project conducting shuttle diplomacy and consensus building with every BU leader. While this overall process took more than six months—which was very long compared to any other e-commerce project—at the end of the day the change was implemented with full support and consensus of all BUs.

—Ritesh Chaturbedi

An Unexpected Buy-in to Set up an Unexpected Team

I had just started my position as the vice president of business development (VP, BD) at a *Fortune* 200 company. I reported directly to the general manager (GM) as part of his executive staff. He had been recently promoted to his position as well and was in the process of building out his team. I had always respected and admired him as both a leader and a manager.

The GM's vision for BD was to split the responsibilities into two departments between two VPs. He had already hired another person to lead one department, and because of my experiences, he asked me to lead the other department. At the time, my entire team consisted of myself and one other person. The GM gave me great latitude to hire additional personnel and build my own team. How could I refuse such an amazing opportunity and offer?

At first, the GM wanted me to report to the other, more experienced VP, who would report to the GM. I had nothing against the other VP, especially as I didn't know him at all yet, however I knew this hierarchy was not good for either the team or the business. I convinced the GM that our two departments had very different needs and operating requirements due to the nature of our respective responsibilities. It would make more sense if we both reported to him directly so he would get both pictures together and could oversee things more holistically. This was not my ego, but what I truly believed would be better for the GM and the business. After some discussion, I was able to get his buy-in, and that call turned out to be more prescient than I could have possibly imagined.

The other VP was a nice person, but professionally, he was not getting the job done. After about six months, the GM had to let him go and asked if I would take over both teams. [Note: this story continues in Chapter 3.]

—Alex Min

Helping Leaders Buy In and Not Lose Their Marbles

Several years ago, I was working with an executive in Africa who was satisfied with the direction his company was taking, yet unsatisfied with the input he was getting from his team. The more we discussed the issue it became clear he was worried that his team felt uncomfortable, and potentially afraid, to speak freely with him. The fact that he was worried about this made it almost certainly true.

During our conversation, he provided stereotypical explanations of his meetings. One-on-one meetings were held in his office with his employees sitting across his desk from him. Team meetings were held in the conference room where he would sit at the head of the table to control the conversations. He acknowledged the physical set up of these meetings could likely be contributing to his issue, and he was still quite reluctant to change what he had become comfortable with.

In response to his reluctance, we quickly shifted the conversation and focused on the improvements he thought he would experience if his people were comfortable opening up in front of him. He smiled as he talked about process improvements, employee development, and his managers taking accountability. Once we had his mind focused on these outcomes we were able to influence him to commit to sitting in the middle of the table during team meetings and coming out from behind his desk to hold one-on-one meetings with no barriers between him and his employees. His final quote at the end of our session was "I'll try it, but they will think I lost my marbles!"

Four months later we reconnected and he was astonished at the difference these changes made. He laughed and said that initially people thought he went mad, but it didn't take long for him to set a new tone with his people. Once they found him more approachable they started to open up. After he rewarded their vulnerability by taking action, they made several critical process changes and started having managers rotate responsibilities for running team meetings. I couldn't help but smile when he said the culture shift he experienced in that short time was like night and day.

—Michael Reddington, CFI, Vice President of Executive Education,
Wicklander-Zulawski and Associates

The Story of 10 Percent: Lead from Where You Stand

I spent several years on active duty as a Naval Officer; I still continue my service in the reserves. I'm proud of my service not only to my country, but also, and sometimes more importantly, to the sailors that I worked with on the ships that I served.

I went to boot camp in Newport, RI, and was assigned to Charlie company and its very own gunnery sergeant. Now, for those of you that have never been in boot camp of met a gunnery sergeant but have watched a few movies on either: well, Hollywood did not make it up.

I was yelled at, got up early, ran until I was sick (literally … and congratulated on getting to that point), did a million sit-ups and push-ups, ran everywhere, and learned the other military motto. The Marines had *Semper Fidelis* or "Always Faithful" while in boot camp we have another motto: *Semper* Gumby or "Always Flexible." We would run everywhere, and then wait—until the mess hall opened, until it was time to go upstairs to our rooms, or just until the gunnery sargeant decided we'd waited enough!

It was a challenging place to be for a 19 year old who thought she knew everything. It was humbling, but it became something else. Throughout the extremely trying days, it was also invigorating. In the evenings, if we had a few minutes of down time between running (and waiting) for the next exercise, gunnery sergeant would sit my 60-plus member Charlie company down and talk to us about what was really ahead of us—what was *not* advertised on the recruitment forms.

For we were all going to be leaders or impact players of our organizations—in some way, every one of us would be leading a ship, a squadron, a platoon at some point, at some level. We would be faced with a variety of challenges—from the basics of developing people to prepare for their next level, the next promotion, or (hopefully) even one day having our employees take our own job (which is a great accomplishment for *any* leader). We would face dealing with difficult people (both above and below, and *at* our level in the organization), deal with challenging bureaucracies, and try to get things done when there were a hundred things to do.

How would we do it? How would we know which one to start first? What if there were a hundred different problems that we recognized when we checked in? How would I know which one to start? What's most important? The more he talked, the more concerned we found ourselves as the gravity of our jobs, as leaders or not, loomed larger by the minute.

And then … he said something that made it all possible. Something, that if you listened, truly listened to what he said, to how he said it—and thought about it in your own words and experiences—you realized you could make it happen.

It was this: **change your 10 percent**. Focus on the areas of your work that you can make a change, make an impact, and let go of the ones that you can't.

Isn't that a little defeatist? Doesn't that basically mean that you are just giving up on areas that needed help—that needed work and your support as well?

No—not at all. I guarantee you when you go off to your next job, your next task, you'll see a number of challenges or problems that you'll want to fix if you haven't already felt it. Have you already been there?

So do it. Don't be afraid. You have the ability to make that impact—to make that change. When I say "change your 10 percent," I want you to focus on your immediate area—where can you make the biggest impact? Impact that area and make it happen.

If you focus on areas that you can't impact (right now)—because you don't have the responsibility level or it's in another department—you could find yourself frustrated and become unmotivated or unengaged. Instead, where could you better spend that time and energy?

Focus on your 10 percent! And you know what? If you focus on your 10 percent, and I focus on my 10 percent, then eventually we will make the impact together.

How do I change my 10 percent?

You're not just a cog in the wheel of a company—you're not just a pebble on the company's road to riches. You have the ability to make an impact in your job right here, right now.

Just an analyst? No way. You are the main person diving into the data, making sense of a bunch of numbers and spreadsheets. No one else is going to look at it the way you do. No one else has the *exact* knowledge, experience, and understanding as you do.

Just a frontline manager? Not a chance. You have the ability to impact others in their professional lives, their personal lives, and their careers. You are an important piece of the puzzle, and perhaps changing your 10 percent means impacting a person that finds a career that sets them on a trajectory they never imagined.

Will you get it wrong? Sure, sometimes. That's fine. In fact, no, that's not fine—that's *great*. If you're not getting it wrong, if you're not applying yourself, challenging yourself, pushing yourself out of the box—you're not doing it right. Thomas Edison once said that "many of life's failures are people who did not realize how close they were to success when they gave up." Push yourself outside of your comfort zone every now and then—you may be surprised just how much is right outside your door.

Don't like what you're doing? That's OK—deal with it. Changing your 10 percent means you know what you have the ability to impact and leave alone the areas you can't change. For some of you that means that although the job you have isn't what you want right now, or in the field of this just-finished, hard-earned degree—with focus, you can find what it is that you do enjoy, you do well, and makes you happy.

If you can't change your job or position right away—then consider this advice: **bloom where you're planted**. It doesn't mean you'll be there forever. But if you're in position now—make the best of it—because you could be amazed at how it gets you where you want to go. Maybe someone will see you do amazing work for a job that was underestimated. Maybe they will notice how hard you work, regardless of what you do. Do great things now, reap the rewards later. Bloom where you're planted.

—*Ashley Prisant Lesko*

CHAPTER 2

Understanding That Change Is Not a Dirty Word

2.1 The SBSG Story

"Step 1 is done," thinks Elizabeth. She is on to the next phase of TEO—preparing for the assessment. At least she thinks so. She knows there are many steps, and this phase will be a challenge because, although it makes sense in theory, it will be the first time she has done it on this scale. She has never prepared for an assessment on this scale before.

She also remembers the last time SBSG rolled out a change. It was a reorganization—the company went from a regional organization (everyone working for one leader in each region) to a matrix organization (one general manager, finance leader, marketing leader, HR leader, loss prevention leader, etc.). It was a good move for the company—and, really, for the employees too—but a disaster in implementation. People fought for months. There was no communication on what was happening (past, present, or future), and employees felt uncertain and unhappy about the results.

Elizabeth wonders if her project will turn out the same way. Is the SBSG culture simply less agreeable to change?

Her goal is to increase productivity in each department involved in the TEO project by 10 percent and to help prepare two of her three leaders to assume more responsibility—ultimately, to move up and take her role or a similar one. She also wants the other 10 people on her team to have more innovative ideas so they are improving one to two areas positively—in some way—every month, on their own.

It is a big wish list. Change stands in the way.

2.2 The Nuts and Bolts

Let's get started. Does that sentence fill you with anticipation? Or a bit of excitement, followed by more dread at the prospect? Or … just dread in general?

Chances are, you're feeling a bit of anxiety about starting a new project. Almost everyone, from experienced project managers to brand new "put in leadership because no one else was there" managers, feels concern over a new project, especially one that imparts change on the group that fights it the most—people.

People inherently struggle with change. The status quo is easier to embrace—it's a known quantity. However, to stay the same is to fall behind. (Just ask Kodak at the onset of digital cameras!) For your organization to move forward, it must improve, interact, and innovate.

This project—your TEO project, where you will help individuals go beyond the job description—will help with all three:

- Improve
- Interact
- Innovate

You just need a few tools to accomplish each. If this is your first time making changes on this scale in your organization, you are in luck. You're not the first to head in this direction—in fact, there's an entire industry devoted to you in change management called organizational development.

Organizational development is a process that improves an organization, or a part of an organization (such as individual or group), through development using specific techniques to increase an organization's effectiveness (Anderson 2015). Almost all organizations go through the process, even if they do not realize it. Those that are successful at organizational development understand that their success with the organizational change will be proportionate to the number of people who support the change and who are what I like to call "along for the ride."

So, let's get the ride started, shall we?

Why People Change

There are two general reasons people change: because they need to (to survive in some way) and because, well, it's human nature (think about the inventions of fire, the printing press, automobiles, and smartphones).

Humans have been transforming themselves since the dawn of time. From caves to our air-conditioned houses, from the wheel to the Jaguar, it is in our innate nature to improve upon what we have. Some may say that better is the enemy of good, but the human race has thrived for thousands of years by changing and improving upon the status quo. Why not be part of the river that runs it?

Survival, though, is also a part of why people change. Consider an organization like Kodak, mentioned earlier, that woke up and realized the digital camera "train" had left the station—and Kodak wasn't on it. The company didn't realize how the market was changing and eventually filed for bankruptcy in 2012. Or take Motorola, which was nearly synonymous with mobile phones; it was entirely eclipsed by a laptop company called Apple.

Change has to happen for us to move forward. You may not be fighting for your next meal, but your organization has to grow. Change has to develop itself, or you run the risk of being left behind.

Why People Don't Change

I know many people, both on a personal or professional level, who will stay in the same town, eat the same five foods, or work in the same job (even though it's making them miserable) because they are afraid of the unknown. We're creatures of habit. Our routine becomes so mindless that we oftentimes don't even realize our own habits.

Change feels hard. That's the reason many give for saying they won't change. But why is change hard? *It takes us out of our comfort zone.* I have no idea what's out there, so I'll stay here. It's familiar and requires minimal effort.

I served active in the Navy for five years, and when I decided to get out, it was one of the hardest decisions. I had no idea what the civilian world was like, and I did not know how I would adjust. Although I worked long hours and was gone months at a time, the Navy was home—it was comfortable, and I knew where I was going. Now I was going where no one knew my name—and no one knew of my accomplishments beyond what I told them. I thought of the movie *The Shawshank Redemption*, in that even after only five years, I felt a bit like the old man who spent his entire life in prison—the outside world was so different.

However, leaving the Navy was a needed change for me—and I thrived after. I had to go out of my comfort zone to do it—and I've been doing it (trying to!) ever since. I will be honest, I do struggle sometimes with something completely radical such as leading a project that I'm not sure of the results, or taking on a new position where I have little to no experience, but I work through it, realizing "you'll never know if you don't go" (from the line in the song "All Star" by Smash Mouth).

Final Note on Change Resistance

While you work on the TEO project, you will find people resistant to change. Read through the rest of the chapter to prepare yourself at the beginning of the project. If you encounter challenges during the project, visit Chapter 8, "Roadblocks," to learn how to handle some of the more commonly occurring challenges.

Nutshell: How Change Management Works

A project that uses change management does so normally for three reasons—to manage natural employee resistance to change (as mentioned above), to increase the chances of success for a given project, and to help reduce the transition time (Hiatt 2017).

Jeff Hiatt, founder of Prosci, created the ADKAR model, a model to evaluate how to implement change in your organization (Hiatt 2004). A short outline is listed in Table 2.1, and additional references are provided at the end of the book. You may find similarities between the model and Elizabeth Kübler-Ross's model five stages of grief. It could also been seen as a transition guide, as it transitions someone through the change.

The goal of the ADKAR model is to help you through the transitions of the change. It offers viewpoints you may not have so you (or others) can transition through. Having the diverse viewpoints can help you transition through the change. By seeing others' viewpoints, you have the ability to envision the transition beyond your own limitations or experiences. Plenty of references and management tools are listed on the Internet and in books that can help you, depending on your situation and desired approach.

The ADKAR model can work well with the DICE model discussed in the next section. You can use the questions suggested in the ADKAR model to form your own change-management process and then use the DICE model to evaluate how successful your project will be.

TABLE 2.1.   The ADKAR Model

	WHAT IT IS	IF YOU DON'T HAVE IT, YOU MAY FIND ...	QUESTIONS TO ASK
Awareness	For the need for change	Confusion	Why is the change needed? What is the nature of the change? What if we don't change?
Desire	For participant, support for change	Resistance	What are employees motivated for in this space? How does the organization drive support?
Knowledge	On how to change	Fear/Worry	What knowledge do employees have to change? How will they be trained on (accepting) the new processes?
Ability	To implement needed skills, behaviors	Frustration	How will we know that the change has worked? How will the employees show capabilities/performance resulting from the change?
Reinforcement	To keep the change in place	Regression	How will we support the change after the project is over? How will we recognize the successes of the project with the employees?

How Successful Will Your TEO Change Management Project Be?

If I could tell you how well you would do before you invest in a project, would you want to hear the answer?

"Heck yeah! Sure," you say. It would be great to find out the result of every project before investing the time and money (and putting yourself out there in front of the leadership team). It would also be nice to have a weather forecast that is right for a day (let alone a week!).

The chapters in this book are designed to guide you through building the most solid plan for implementing your TEO project. Remember, you're not an island. Ask for help. Let others know what you're doing—and where you are in the project. Communicate, socialize, network. How many times have we heard that it's not always about *what* we know but also *who* we know?

Although no forecasting model is 100 percent accurate, one model can help you predict the outcome of your project before it starts: the DICE model. It requires you to calculate a score for each of the model's four factors (see Tables 2.2 and 2.3). If the score is not what you want it to be, the creators of the model provide suggestions on how to improve to give yourself a greater probability of success (Sirkin, Keenan, and Jackson 2005). To determine how successful your change management project will be, evaluate it on these four factors:

- *Duration.* How long the project will take, or time between milestones.
- *Integrity.* How well the team that is implementing the project can complete it when/how/where the team said it could.
- *Commitment.* This involves the level of commitment given by both executives (C1) and the employees being affected by the change (C2).
- *Effort.* How much work is required of employees above normal requirements due to the project.

2.3 Activities and Application

DICE in Application

Below is a brief evaluation of a DICE analysis in action. Read the questions below and insert the score for each in the boxes provided. The score for each should be between 1 and 4 (1 is "highly likely to contribute to the project's success," whereas 4 is "highly unlikely to contribute to the project's success"). For more information, please refer to the article listed in the reference section.

TABLE 2.2.   DICE

TOPIC	SCORE
Duration (D)	
Integrity (I)	
Commitment from executives (C1)	
Commitment from employees (C2)	
Effort (E)	

TABLE 2.3.   Question Evaluation Table

TOPIC/QUESTIONS	SCORE
Duration (D) Do formal project reviews occur regularly? If the project needs to take more than two months to complete, what is the average time between reviews?	1 point—time between project reviews < 2 months 2 points—time between project reviews 2–4 months 3 points—time between project reviews 4–8 months 4 points—time between project reviews > 8 months
Integrity (I) Is team leader capable? How strong are team members' skills and motivations? Do they have sufficient time to spend on the change initiative?	1 point—team led by strong, capable leader; members have correct skills, motivation to finish project in time frame; company has >50% team member's time with project 2–3 points—team has 1–4 capabilities under "1 point" 4 points—team is lacking everything in "1 point"
Commitment from executives (C1) Do senior executives regularly communicate the reason for the change and the importance of its success? Is message convincing? Is message consistent, both across top management team and over time? Has top management devoted enough resources to the change program?	1 point—executives have clearly communicated the need for change through actions and words 2–3 points—executives appear to be neutral to change 4 points—executives appear to be reluctant to support change
Commitment from employees (C2) Do the employees most affected by the change understand the reason for it and believe it's worthwhile? Are they enthusiastic and supportive or worried and obstructive?	1 point—employees eager to take on change initiative 2 points—employees are willing to take on change initiative 3 points—employees are reluctant 4 points—employees are strongly reluctant

TOPIC/QUESTIONS	SCORE
Effort (E) What is the percentage of increased effort that employees must give to implement the change effort? Does the incremental effort come on top of a heavy workload? Have people strongly resisted the increased demands on them?	1 point—project requires <10% extra work by employees 2 points—10-20% extra work 3 points—20-40% extra work 4 points—>40% extra work

*Questions from Sirkin, Keenan, and Jackson 2005.

DICE Count

Now take the scores from above and insert them in the equation below:

$$\text{DICE Score} = D + (2 * I) + (2 * C1) + C2 + E$$

Results: When you calculate the results, the outcome could range from an outstanding 7 to a not-so-productive 28. Based on the researchers' results, you should expect the following with your score:

- **Scores between 7 and 14:** Voted most likely to succeed. Called the "Win Zone."
- **Scores between 14 and 17**: The project can be done, but you should be increasingly concerned as the score approaches 16. This zone is also known as the "Worry Zone."
- **Scores between 17 and 28:** Ouch. This is a chancy project, and the odds for success are fairly low; the project will more than likely fail. Called the "Woe Zone."

2.4 Real Stories

New Spaces, Bigger Changes

Small changes can disrupt; large changes can derail. A few years ago, we moved office locations from a conveniently located, quiet office park to a congested area with lots of buzz in order to improve our corporate profile and visibility. I thought everyone would be ecstatic to have great food options, a vibrant, glitzy office space, and access to nice amenities. Wow, was I off-base! I was not tuned into my colleagues' concerns. Several co-workers were going to experience significant increases in commute times, and there were concerns with safety issues in the parking garage and misgivings about migrating from private offices to an open office layout.

What did we do? Though I was late to interpreting the signals, my co-workers huddled and discussed the trade-offs from leaving a food desert in a tired business park to a vibrant, active area of the city. The project leader within our office created excitement among our team by talking about the layout, the cool new look and vision for the office, and how the new space would promote better opportunities to collaborate. I failed to articulate my vision and reasoning, but my colleagues stepped up to fill in my gaps. Slowly, as with any big change, my teammates warmed up to the notion of moving and embraced the new space. Now people wonder why we did not do it sooner because we have better connectivity, talent recruitment, and quality of life. I am proud we accomplished many of the business objectives we outlined as part of the move, but I learned a lot about tapping into people's fears and concern for uncertainty.

If change is a constant in an organization, it is less likely to disrupt a team because they are more practiced in adaptability. However, if you make a big change in a stable environment, it tends to really destabilize the entire group. It is imperative to make big change slowly, and practice small changes frequently so people are more receptive to being nimble. Most importantly, communicate, communicate, communicate—be clear about what you want to accomplish because people will fill in their own assumptions where there is a lack of clarity.

—*Ben Wilhelm, President Southeast Region, Shiel Sexton Company*

Understanding Change by Establishing Processes

Within the last year, I was working with an organization that was earning $3 million in annual revenue, but likely had the potential to earn at least $10 million. They had a very strong core base of clients, some transient clients, and were having a little difficulty consistently penetrating new markets. They had a passionate and knowledgeable team. Their sales process presented the first glaring opportunity.

The opportunity was so large because, simply put, there wasn't an established process. They had multiple representatives selling to the same clients, they lacked a centralized communication strategy and they weren't consistently tracking their efforts. The lack of a clear process meant they could only react to the results they experienced, which could be misleading.

Through a series of meetings, we highlighted the strengths of the organization while focusing on the potential revenue that could be realized. This solution-oriented mindset allowed us to create a sales process where every representative was responsible for creating a detailed annual and quarterly action plan. These plans were reinforced and adjusted through monthly accountability calls. Additionally, the sales process was enhanced by shifting to an educational sales approach. In the first year, including the rollout and training process, they experienced a sales increase of $600,000.

—*Michael Reddington, CFI, Vice President of Executive Education,*
Wicklander-Zulawski and Associates

Understanding Change through Partnership That May Not Be What You Expected

Even with more than 25 years of leadership experience, I still have the desire to learn and grow, even though it may mean a tough lesson every now and then. However, being an optimistic person, I try very hard to get as much as I can and see the benefits of every situation.

After 18 years, I decided it was time to change jobs and look for new challenges and opportunities. I found a job that would allow me to focus more on strategic planning and operational strategies and less on day-to-day responsibilities. I looked forward to the opportunities and meeting new people, but as my orientation progressed I found myself in a situation that I had not recently experienced and did not have all the knowledge that my subordinates had. In a new healthcare setting, I found myself in a terrain of unfamiliar regulations and mandates.

I knew little about state and federal rules or the reimbursement structure, yet I landed in an office with poor processes, minimal growth, and financial struggles. The staff was content but the organizational leaders knew things had to change and needed me to go in and get them on the right track. The new manager knew the rules and regulations and had a commitment for doing the right thing, but what she lacked was organizational theory and HR management skills. Together, she and I found an eagerness and desire to learn from each other and both of us were quick studies.

In a matter of six weeks, I grew in my regulatory proficiency while she developed processes and gained knowledge and confidence in managing staff and day-to-day responsibilities. While initially uncomfortable, I attempted to share my knowledge while learning from a subordinate and ended up with two stronger people. Those individuals developed two of their colleagues that were able to offer even more to the organization.

—*Jeanie Stoker, MPA, RN, BSN, BC*

CHAPTER 3

What Cards Are in Your Hand? Knowing What Your Employees Have Helps You Know How Best to Stack the Deck

3.1 The SBSG Story

Joe sighs, turns his desk chair to face the window, and gazes outside. As VP of operations, he is always looking to improve—so he was initially glad to have Elizabeth's ideas to improve the department as well as potentially influence a change in SBSG.

But is this too much, too quickly?

He has been with the majority of the members of this team for a short while—only about a year. He doesn't know them very well since most of his work has either him or them traveling—and not at the same time. How would he get to know them and know how to help them? Elizabeth is good, but she hasn't been leading long. He views his job as multitasking—he needs to be helping her while helping the rest of the team so they can continue working on the "good" problem of following the hockey-stick (quick-expansion) growth plan for SBSG for the next three to five years.

Is there a way that he can get to know the team members, an easy way that will help him understand what makes them tick so he can also provide perspective? He needs to do this not only for the team, but also for Tyler, the CEO, whose primary goal for cutting costs is to limit hiring for growth by increasing productivity. Is it possible?

3.2 The Nuts and Bolts

Congratulations. You have passed the first few (but by no means the easiest) wickets on your road to having the most talent-engaged and productive crew you've had—you've secured buy-in from the executive team, you have defined your team's current state, and you have an idea of how you want the team to look in 100 days. Or, maybe you have only about 85 days now, since it probably took at least two weeks to get on the executive's schedule and to reach this point in the program. (I get it. Executives are hard sometimes!)

You've learned a little about organizational development and the basics of change management, which can be tools for you to use as you work with your team, regardless if you're in HR or not. It doesn't matter if you even realized that organizational development existed—you were probably already using some of the principles without knowing it. As you continue in this book, you'll realize the same is true for talent engagement—you may have delved into it as well.

Now it's time to start doing some real work. Time to roll up your sleeves and get to the good part—helping your employees do more, with the assets they already have but aren't using.

What You Need to Assess—Using Assessments to Understand Who You Have on the Team

You may have 2, 5, 20, 50, or more people on your team. They are each different in so many ways. Some you know but others are not as familiar to you. Briefly describe the normal ways that you get to know people on your team. Note that "team" can also include people other than direct reports, such as in a project team with peers or senior individuals.

If you do not have a repeated process for getting to know individuals on your team (such as a checklist, an assessment, or a one-on-one meeting), feel free to do an Internet search and pick the method that best works for you, your line of work, and the individuals on your team. You'll have more opportunity in Part 3.3 to develop your thoughts, but for now, jot down a few notes.

_____

_____

_____

_____

_____

_____

_____

_____

_____

_____

_____

_____

_____

_____

_____

_____

_____

_____

_____

When many officers first join the Navy as an ensign, they become a division officer. I was a division officer on two ships—a destroyer and cruiser—and had titles such as navigator and gunnery officer. I was typically assigned a group of sailors numbering between 10 and 30—in all ranks, experiences, and ages. I quickly had to get to know them and figure out how best to motivate and engage them.

Getting to know your team does not have to be difficult. One of my favorite ways to do that was by completing a simple form called a division officer's notebook or "Divo notebook" for each person (US Navy 2007). It's a checklist that is set up as a form (we military folks love our checklists and forms!)—where each person had been, what he or she had done, and then areas to help you figure out what each person could do. Effective department heads (the manager of the division officer), could help guide you through some of the most important questions. If not … well, you were on your own.

Completing each form wasn't always easy, but it was possible. The Divo notebook was one way to learn information, facts, and data points about an individual. Although it was a framework for getting information, it by no means cut out the need to get to know each team member on a personal level. At the end of the day, you have to get to know your people. You have to take the time to learn—in some way or another. The Divo notebook was a start. Talking to your people is a start. Using the information that you wrote down above about how you get to know your staff is a start. The better you know your team members, the better you can assess their abilities and give them more of what they need or want so that *you* can get more of what you need or want (for the team or company). A colleague of mine, Greg Slamowitz, who spends a lot of time maximizing job satisfaction for individuals, said that one of things you should want to do is to get people to the top of Maslow's pyramid. The higher they are, the more they are contributing in their job, company, and organization.

But first, where are you?

Maslow—the Man, the Myth, the Legend

Maslow's hierarchy of needs (Figure 3.1) is an example of an assessment that tracks our progress toward self-actualization, or what I call "the best me I can be." In 1943, Abraham Maslow built the stages a person has to climb in order to grow or be that "best me." Maslow defined the highest level—self-actualization—as the point where "what a man can be, he must be"(Barnes 2000).

An employee is typically expected to spend 40 hours working (out of 168 total hours in a week), give or take a few hours. Therefore, a person's career is a significant enough portion of one's life to influence where he or she is in the hierarchy.

For example, the lowest level on the hierarchy is physiological needs. This level highlights the bare minimum of human survival, which includes food, clothing, and shelter. Physiological needs could be influenced by your work compensation—how much you get paid. Your compensation (which could also include benefits) will translate into fulfilling you and your family's basic needs.

As you move up in the pyramid, the more in control you may feel of your career, the more motivated you are to do what you are doing, and the more you may be able to recognize your strengths and values and be able to give back to others from those strengths.

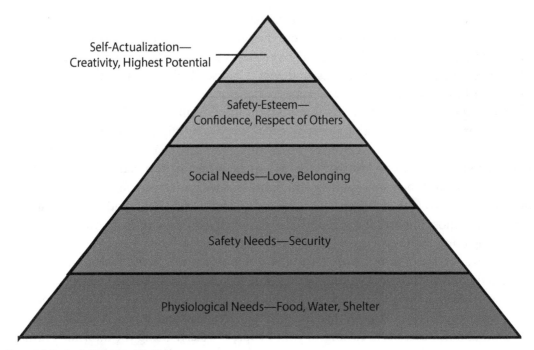

Figure 3.1. Maslow's Heirarchy of Needs

SO HOW DOES THE WORKPLACE INFLUENCE AN INDIVIDUAL'S LIFE THROUGH MASLOW'S HIERARCHY?

Work provides the basics for an individual's needs—through pay and benefits that the organization offers. Based on the culture of the workplace and one's work-life balance, the workplace influences the employee's feeling of safety, belonging, and esteem (that is, being valued and recognized).

SO WHAT DO WE DO WITH THIS INFORMATION?

If you and I are challenging ourselves to motivate employees beyond their job description, we have to set a favorable, conducive work environment. We will later dive much deeper into individual motivation and needs, but in a general sense promoting a positive work environment could include focusing on areas that help your employees be the best they can be—by clearing out the junk of the job. For instance, we could reduce meeting times, make meetings more efficient, revisit current processes, and identify opportunities to reach the same or higher goal with focus on employees satisfaction.

Why You Need to Assess Your Team

So you may have some basic understanding of your team members, and you may know where they are and where they are going, which is great!

But what if you don't? What if you don't have the time? For instance, you have a brand-new team starting, and you know the team may have issues, such as working together, gaining trust, or getting tasks done on time, but you need it to run a building in three months.

This scenario, in which you don't have the time to really dig in to what makes your team tick, happens frequently. Enter the opportunity to assess your team.

Assessments have been around for hundreds of years. One definition of an assessment is an "educational measurement"—something to measure how much or what a person knows, feels, or believes about a certain topic (Wilbrink 1997). Assessments help people gauge where they are, as individuals, in reference to others. Assessments also help determine types, styles, direction, and values based on choices people make during the assessments.

I look at assessments as a shortcut to learn more about your people—and getting to where you want to go a little faster. Since you are probably smarter than most (you are reading this book, after all), you know you need to get in the details—knowing your people, understanding the needs of your business with the skills of your people—but time is not always your friend. Using a proven assessment can help you understand the nuances of others quickly. Most assessments will also help you in applying your employees' assessment results to help the organization; for example, CliftonStrengths (fomerly StrengthsFinder), Myers-Briggs Type Indicator (MBTI), and Talent Engagement Zone offer activities and application suggestions upon completion to both the individuals assessed and the administrator of the assessment.

Why Is Knowing What Motivates My People Important?

Great question. I thought you'd never ask. Brainstorm for a second. Answer a simple question. Quickly, off the top of your head—what motivates you? List three to five items.

_____

_____

_____

_____

_____

_____

_____

Look at the list above. How do you use the items at work?

_____

_____

_____

_____

_____

_____

_____

_____

Have you ever had a bad boss who did not help motivate you? What more could you have done if he or she had motivated you more?

_____

_____

_____

_____

_____

_____

_____

_____

OK, so there you have it. If your manager had motivated you … you could have done more, wanted to do more, and volunteered to do more. So let's learn about what motivates your team members to do more.

Why Is Motivation Important?

There are two kinds of motivation—intrinsic and extrinsic. *Intrinsic motivation* is the kind that comes—yes, you guessed it—internally. You do it because you want to, because it makes you feel good, and because it's a challenge. You don't necessarily need someone to pat you on the back and say you've done a good job. You can be driven by both intrinsic and *extrinsic motivation* at the same time. Extrinsic motivation gives you energy—the drive to do more—based on your external environment. For example, your boss recognizes you in front of the entire department for a job well done on a project. You get a raise or a promotion. Someone or something has given you recognition—and that is motivation for you.

Now, take a look at your answers to the question of what motivates you. How quickly were you able to answer that question? Let's say your boss walks in the door right now and says to you, "You're going to a new job." This job will have *none* of the work motivation items on your list. What's more, you may lose other factors that motivate you, such as more time with your family.

Here's a basic fact. People do what they do based on motivation. Good or bad, motivation drives what we do every day. In the context of this book, and your TEO project, the assessments you use to find out more about the individuals on your team are examining their motivators. Find out what motivates them, and you'll increase their engagement (Lesko 2015).

Giving Them More of What They Want Helps Them Grow

Research has proven that giving individuals more of what motivates them increases their engagement—by as much as 25 percent (Lesko 2015). It is not simply a matter of wanting what motivates you (which sounds like an oxymoron, doesn't it?), but it is also about having what you really need and want—whether you're a manager or a frontline employee. Think back to Maslow's pyramid. The more I am able to contribute and to be held in high esteem (in the eyes of both myself and potentially my peers), the more

I am using my strengths, and the closer I can reach self-actualization—truly being all I can be.

Employees are not robots. They are not their job descriptions (you know this part already). For example, you may hire John to fill the description of accountant, but John is changing. He may be only a few years out of college when you hire him, but he changes as the years go on. He can now do more, understand more, and give more than what's required of him to do the standard job description. Assuming he does not change jobs or roles, he has the ability to benefit from hearing the perspectives of his team and manager. How do you tap into that experience and skill set—for his benefit *and* yours and your organization's?

On the flip side, John knows a lot more than when he started, and he realizes he can work a lot less if he wants. He finds that after a few years, he can turn in a report on Thursday that was due Tuesday—and no one notices. He cuts corners and leaves a few pages off a report, citing being overworked as the cause. As a result, he, with his learned knowledge, can now argue that he needs another person on his team, to help do the work that at one time (when he first started) he could do on his own. (Your TEO project will help you solve these problems ... read on!)

Assessing your individuals, especially on a periodic basis, *takes a pulse* of where your employees are, what they want, and potentially where they want to go. It helps you see some of the issues they may have below the surface—such as lagging job completion or challenges with other individuals or teams, and with more development, they can avoid the lack of interest at work. They can build on their talents—and you can align their talents with your goals and your company goals.

Choosing an Assessment

If you had a nickel for every assessment you've ever taken or for every time someone has said, "Oh, I think this one will solve your problems," you'd have what ... a dollar? Two dollars? Ten dollars?

There are a lot of assessments to choose from. You'll need to review them to figure out which one is best. First, you have to pick the right method that will answer these questions: What, specifically, do you want to assess? What is your desired outcome or goal?

We'll briefly discuss what you should think about when choosing an assessment. Actual assessments are described in Part 3.3, "Activities and Application."

Checklist: How to Assess What You Need

What's important? What are the top things that you want to find out about your people? What are your priorities?

_____

_____

_____

_____

_____

_____

_____

_____

_____

_____

What is the goal of the assessment? What are you trying to accomplish? (Note: This could be "I want to know more about my people," "I want to know what motivates them, what makes them productive," or "I just want to understand them." Think a little about each one of these. In your perfect world—what would your team look like? Now, what information do you need to get that team? Start there.)

_____

_____

_____

_____

_____

_____

_____

_____

_____

What are your limitations? (What prevents you from that perfect-world situation above?). If an item is a limitation, explain in the box provided what the limitation is and why.

	LIMITATION	WHY
Time, Executive		
Time, Manager		
Time, Employee		
Money Per Project		
Money Per Project		
Ability, Analysis		
Ability, Strength of employee understanding		
Ability, Level of employee engagement		
Culture of company, team		
Other (list here)		

Of the limitations above, which will be the most difficult to overcome?

_____

_____

_____

_____

_____

_____

How can the limitation(s) be accommodated? Think outside the box here if needed!

_____

_____

_____

_____

_____

Whose help or buy-in do you need to move forward with the assessment? How can you get that approval? (See also Chapter 1.)

_____

_____

_____

_____

_____

_____

As mentioned, a number of assessment types are listed in Part 3.3. The rankings do not take in the total cost (which could vary based on number of employees, products, and use of consultants) or the amount or type of analysis needed, but they do address each?

Ways of Assessing

The following are different ways that you can assess your team, ranked by amount of time it takes for each assessment technique alone. See Table 3.1 for a summary.

TABLE 3.1.   Resource Assessment Comparison

	BASICS/DIY	INTERVIEWS	ASSESSMENTS
Amount of time	Low—Medium	High	Low
Cost	Low	Medium	Medium—High
Analysis review needs	Medium	High	Low
Depth/richness of analysis information	Medium	High	Low—Medium

1. **The Basics—Do It Yourself (DIY)**
    For those who don't have the money, but have the time, or for those who don't have the money, and really don't have the time but will make it work—this option

is for you. Think of the Home and Garden Channel. A typical show starts with the decorators or designers looking at the basics of a home project, with the elements they have to offer, and figuring out a way to work from there.

That is exactly what you have the ability to do. Remember, the goal of the assessment is to gather information about your team—to learn beyond the basic elements of individuals' job descriptions and to tap into their resources that you aren't using yet. There are two ways that you can do this: through one-on-one meetings (one-on-ones) and development of your own strength list.

a. **Using One-on-One Meetings—The Old-Fashioned Way**
    The one-on-one meeting has been happening for a long time—and yet, it is still not being properly vetted, taken advantage of, and used in a way to help both the manager and leader.

    The purpose of the one-on-one is to dig into the person's value system, their characteristic levels of motivation that make them want to do great things for your company, or that just make them want to show up. Your purpose in using this is an ongoing one—one-on-ones should be held as frequently as possible.

    Other areas to get one-on-one questions include peers at work, internet searches, and industry magazines.

    Where else could you get great one-on-one questions?

    _____

    _____

    _____

    _____

    _____

    _____

    _____

b. **Developing Your Own Strengths, Values, and Talents List**
    More than likely, your company has a mission statement, a vision statement, and maybe even a list of leadership values that is part of the culture of the organization. Instead of reaching out for someone else's assessment that is designed on their set of values and setup of research—why don't you use what you already have?

2. **Interviewing—"You can ask them?"**
    Similar to a one-on-one in that you have to have a conversation with people is the interview method. However, a one-on-one is a direct method and is normally driven by the junior individual—what is on their mind, what is driving them, what resources they need, and how they are progressing to their goals.

In an interview, the person that is seeking information is the one asking the questions. It can be to an individual or a group. It can be the same set of questions to all (which is suggested, to keep continuity) or it can be different, based on the responses (both are acceptable interview techniques). The goal of the interview is to gather information about various people—not just your team but others as well—to formalize information in a logical way, such as emerging trends, issues or problems. This assessment can be time-consuming, as you must first interview and then parse a significant amount of data, but it can be rewarding and cost saving if budget is an issue.

3. **Assessment—A Lot of Knowledge, and Fast**
   The final method is one that allows for the least guesswork and the least amount of time. There are tens if not hundreds of assessments to help with leadership—you just have to pick which one you want. That is easier said than done. For assessments such as the Myers-Briggs Type Indicator (MBTI) to Gallup's CliftonStrengths (formerly StrengthsFinders), the output is only as good as the input—and someone in your organization must determine if the output is what is required to improve the talent on your team. I once led a group that received 20–30 or more new employees *a week* (the organization itself sometimes received up to 1,000 new employees in a week). I didn't have time to conduct one-on-ones (although I would have liked to); I barely even had time to learn their names (unfortunately!). Using an assessment—where I could have a standardized approach to learning a lot about a number of people in a short amount of time—would have helped me better lead the group using the information they had provided about themselves. Some people will lean on an assessment as a guideline, a rulebook, or a bible for their organization. I think no assessment is perfect—but I do think an assessment can be a great tool to help you engage your team's talents. Use them if you can—and proceed with caution!

3.3 Activities and Application

There are a lot of assessments out there. Indeed, if you type "[any word in the English language]" and "assessment" into an Internet search engine, you will probably find one to assess it. Some are better than others. The quality of an assessment depends on when you are taking it and why. Is someone making you take an assessment for an area that you know you won't change, such as using a leadership style that your company's culture does not currently use? Are you desperately looking for the next career change, but you don't know what that change should be? I took an assessment whose results I completely disagreed with—only to take it a few years later and think it was the best thing since sliced bread.

Given the differences between assessments and their relevance to your situation, the assessments listed below are recommendations. I have endeavored to give you a high-level description of each, including their pros and cons. If you haven't read Part 3.2 ("The Nuts and Bolts"), then I would encourage you to review it in conjunction to support your understanding and to make you feel confident that you've chosen the right assessment for you.

The Basics—Do It Yourself (DIY)

ONE-ON-ONE MEETINGS

The one-on-one meeting is held between a manager and employee. The goals for each session can range from goal setting to career development to resource allocation to conflict management.

In terms of talent engagement, the purpose of each one-on-one is to learn more about your employees, for example, what they want to do or what they've done before. What is their purpose for being in their position? What would they like to get out of it? How do they feel they could contribute more to the organization?

One of the challenges for one-on-ones is simply the amount of time they take away from the rest of your schedule. Although these meetings are more important than many other tasks (since they directly impact the future of your team's goals), it is hard to set aside the time to meet with each individual. I once took over a department and immediately had over 50 direct reports. Spending an average of 30 minutes with each would have totaled 25 hours—over 60 percent of one week! That may not be possible to do in a month—but maybe in a quarter.

Table 3.2 is a guideline for the number of one-on-ones you should have based on the number of *direct reports* you have. The recommended amount of time (30 minutes), level, topics, and intensity may vary, but the table should serve as a starting point as you set up the one-on-ones to get more acquainted with your team.

TABLE 3.2. Suggested Number of One-on-Ones for a Leader to Have with Direct Reports

NUMBER OF DIRECT REPORTS	FREQUENCY OF ONE-ON-ONES	MAXIMUM HOURS SPENT (PER MONTH)	PERCENTAGE OF TOTAL HOURS/MONTH
1–3	Weekly	6	4
4–8	Biweekly	8	5
9–15	Monthly	8	5
16–40	Bimonthly	10	6
41–65	Quarterly	10	6
65–120	Biannually	10	6
121–250	Annually	10	6

ONE-ON-ONE QUESTIONS

For managers new to having one-on-one meetings with employees, picking the right questions can be a matter of trial and error, talking to the right mentor, or finding them on your own. Below is a list of questions to get you started in finding out what your employees most want (some questions taken from Cahill 2016, a helpful resource):

TALENT ENGAGEMENT

- How are you currently using your skills and talents in this position?
- If you could work on anything in the next quarter, what would it be? Why?

- What is one thing that I, the team, or the organization could do to make what you do more satisfying? Why?
- At what point in the past month were you most frustrated with or discouraged by work? What can I as a manager or what can your team do to help you manage that?
- What sort of resources could you use to help make things more manageable?
- What can I do to help you enjoy work more or remove roadblocks to progress?
- Which areas would you like more or less guidance from me on work?

JOB ENGAGEMENT

- On a scale of 1–10, how happy are you with your job? What makes you say that?
- What skills, talents, and interests do you have to contribute to the projects you're currently working on? Why?
- What are your most and least favorite areas about work right now?
- What's working well for you in your current job?
- Within the company, department, or team, what is the biggest opportunity we're missing out on, or what areas could we improve upon?

CAREER ENGAGEMENT

- Do you feel as if you're growing in your role? What are the drivers?
- Think back through jobs that you've had; what are some of the work projects you're proudest of, and if given the chance, what would you like to do next?
- Think about your career; what are two or three skills you'd like to learn on the job? What about those skills interests you?
- What other roles or positions could you see yourself in? Are they in this department, team, or company? What areas would you like to explore?
- If you had the chance to create your ideal position, what would it look like? How is it different from what you're doing now? What would you need to get there?
- What goals at work would you like to accomplish in the next 6 to 12 months, and what makes you say that?

THE VALUES LIST

When thinking about the final state or end goal of your talent engagement project—getting more out of your team—ask yourself these question about your team, your department, and your company:

What values, strengths, and talents do you currently have on your team? In your company?

_____

_____

_____

_____

_____

_____

What values, strengths, and talents do you want to have more of on your team? In your company?

_____

_____

_____

_____

_____

Turning the question back to yourself—what strengths, tasks, and talents from your previous job(s) do you miss and would like to use more of now?

_____

_____

_____

_____

_____

Armed with the information above, you will be prepared to work through them as an assessment in Part 3.3. Sometimes it may be helpful to visualize a list of values, strengths, and talents, so a partial list is given in Table 3.3.

Your lists of additional strengths:

_____

_____

_____

_____

_____

TABLE 3.3.   List of Values, Strengths, and Talents in the Workplace

Accurate	Counseling	Focused	Leadership	Precise
Action oriented	Courageous	Friendly	Learning	Presentation Skills
Activating	Creating	Gathering information	Listening	Priority Setting
Adapting	Creativity	Generating ideas	Locating	Problem-solving
Administering	Critical thinking	Generous	Logical	Questioning
Adventurous	Curiosity	Giving feedback	Managing	Repairing
Advising	Dealing with Ambiguity	Gratitude	Marketing	Reporting
Ambitious	Deciding	Helping	Meeting people	Researching
Analytical	Dedicated	Humorous	Mentoring	Resolving

Analyzing information	Detailing	Idealistic	Monitoring	Responsible
Appreciative	Determined	Imagining	Motivating Others	Self-assured
Approachability	Developing people	Implementing	Negotiating	Selling
Artistic	Directing	Independent	Observant	Speaking
Authentic	Disciplined	Influencing	Open minded	Spontaneous
Balancing	Discovering	Informing	Optimistic	Straightforward
Briefing	Educated	Ingenuity	Organized	Strategic thinking
Budgeting	Empathetic	Initiating	Originality	Tactful
Building Effective Teams	Empowering	Innovating	Outgoing	Team oriented
Caring	Energetic	Inspiring	Overseeing	Time Management
Checking	Entertaining	Instructing	Patient	Training
Coaching	Enthusiastic	Integrity	Peer Relationships	Trustworthy
Comfort Around Higher Management	Evaluating	Intelligent	People skills	Understanding Others
Communicative	Explaining	Interpersonal Savvy	Perseverance	Versatile
Compassionate	Fairness	Interviewing	Persistent	Visionary
Confident	Fast	Judging	Personal Learning	Written communication
Conflict Management	Finding	Kindness	Persuasive	
Considerate	Fixing	Knowledgeable	Planning	
Coordinating	Flexible	Launching	Practical	

Interviewing—"You can ask them?"

Some results of interviewing could be discovering emerging trends, issues, or problems—ones you may or may not see right now. Think of it this way: You're an investigator, and you're trying to uncover information that can lead to a treasure (you get to decide what the treasure is since this is your story). The people you are interviewing have the information. How do you find out what they know?

- **Build rapport.** Many people need to be warmed up—have a little prediscussion before the interviewing or fact-finding starts. What are their interests? What is the family like? What's on their desk at work? Ask questions. Encourage them to open up.
- **Help them understand why they are here.** Put them at ease. Are they getting fired? No ... but they may not know that. Explain the meeting's purpose: "Julie, I appreciate you taking the time today to talk to me. I'm really trying to learn a bit more about you. I'm working on a project called TEO [explain as needed] with the goal of helping you get more out of your job—every day. So I'm working on learning more about your interests so we can see how we can better support you in our organization."

- **Ask questions.** What do they want to do in the workplace? What have they done before that they don't get to do now? You can pull from Table 3.3—the list of values and strengths—to help guide the conversation
- **Listen.** Yep. The hard one. What are they saying? You may not know what's important right away—so listen even more intently.
- **Take notes.** Unless you're Sheldon from *The Big Bang Theory* and have an eidetic mind, figure out how you're going to record the information so you can use it later. I use a notepad and tell them I'll take notes (and that it's not a bad thing!).
- **Listen some more.** Nine times out of ten you won't do it enough. Just listen. They should talk 75–80 percent of the time.
- **Create the follow-up—you, them, or otherwise.** If this is a regularly scheduled one-on-one and you're the manager, you can let them follow up, if that's your way of doing so. If the meeting is just for your TEO project, let them know the next steps. Communicate what will happen with the information, if needed. The next chapter talks about analyzing data collected, so if you gather research for that, you can save it for when we review Chapter 4.

Assessment—Gathering a Lot of Knowledge, and Fast

You've made the decision to purchase an assessment tool, great. You have been able to put some money into the decision, and you want fast, accurate information.

Now which one do you purchase?

The final method we discuss here—the use of assessments—is one that allows for the least guesswork and the least amount of time. There are tens if not hundreds of assessments to help with leadership—you just have to pick which one you want. That is easier said than done.

For assessments, such as the Myers-Briggs Type Indicator (MBTI) and Gallup's CliftonStrengths, the output is only as good as the input—and someone in your organization must determine if the output is what is required to improve the talent on your team. Some people will lean on an assessment as a guideline, a rulebook, or a bible for their organization. I think no assessment is perfect—but I do think an assessment can be a great tool to help you engage your team's talents. Use them if you can—and proceed with caution!

Table 3.4 displays information on the most used assessments and makes recommendations based on a variety of characteristics. Note that most are one-size-fits-all and do not have much room to be customized to your company culture or needs. If you need something that is more tailored to your company, I would recommend following one of the previously mentioned assessment methods (DIY or interviewing) or working with a consultant to meet your needs.

Each one of these is a valuable assessment in its own right, but you may have to review their results and compare them with what you want and need (remember those questions you answered earlier?). You may not need to pick the most expensive or the most popular—pick the one that best matches your and your organization's needs.

TABLE 3.4.   Assessments Analysis

ASSESSMENT	COST PER ITEM ($)	MEASURES	APPLICATION	STRENGTHS	WEAKNESSES	USE IF YOU:	FOR ADDITIONAL INFORMATION
CliftonStrengths (formerly Strengths Finder)	16	Top 5 talents/ strengths	Help employees understand and maximize use of strengths/ talents to increase engagement in workplace	Easy to understand and use; developed by Gallup, from 40-plus years of research; additional workbook provided online	Must buy assessment for each individual; additional training may be necessary; executive support for program to be most effective	Need a fast, reliable report on employee strengths and want to take a shortcut in learning about a group of people	http://strengths. gallup.com
Talent Engagement Zone	0	Number of individual's talents/ strengths used in workplace	Understand individual's best use/ application of strengths in current job	Quick; easy to understand; free; applicable data to use immediately	Starting point; needs to be paired with another assessment	Know your strengths and want to find ways to use them; want to understand opportunity to grow in job	http:// squarepeg solutions.org
Reflected Best Self Exercise	9-15	Understanding of individual's best strengths based on other's viewpoints	Feedback-based exercise to understand strengths based on others' perspectives	Positive assessment; nearly all results are confidence- and esteem-building items; unique 360-degree look at individual through feedback and stories	Assessment can be relative and is subjective based on input from individuals selected for feedback; somewhat time-consuming for individual and others giving feedback	Want a positive strengths model; have individuals who have ability to reflect on information shared by others	http:// positiveorgs. bus.umich. edu/cpo-tools/ reflected-best-self-exercise-2nd-edition
Success Scale	0	Work optimism; positive engagement; support provision	Understand how to creative positive growth and predicting success at work	Quick; easy to understand; free; applicable data to use immediately	Starting point; may need another assessment; depending on goals, may need additional support or training to carry out objectives	Want to develop culture and understand positive side of strengths; need to quantify positive engagement at work	http:// broadcasting happiness.com/ success-scale
Utrecht Work Engagement Scale (UWES)	0	Level of work engagement	Understand work engagement of an employee in 3 areas: vigor, dedication, absorption	Short, 9- or 17-question assessment to understand work engagement in 3 areas that can be assessed individually (for example, vigor) or as as whole (work engagement); alternate to employee engagement survey	May need another assessment to understand what to do with the information provided	Need to get a starting-point gauge of your employees in work/ employee engagement	http://www. wilmarschaufeli. nl/publications/ Schaufeli/ Test%20 Manuals/Test_ manual_UWES_ English.pdf

ASSESSMENT	COST PER ITEM ($)	MEASURES	APPLICATION	STRENGTHS	WEAKNESSES	USE IF YOU:	FOR ADDITIONAL INFORMATION
Career Anchors	20–40	Top motivating factors at work for individual	Uses 8 anchors to better understand what motivates individual in a specific job	Specifc results of assessment lead to actionable items; for example, these items motivate individuals so the more they have them, the more they will be engaged	More expensive assessment; additional training may be necessary	Need to understand specific motivation areas to help get employees in the right place at work	https://www.careeranchorsonline.com/SCA/about.do?open=prod
Myers-Briggs Type Indicator (MBTI)	0	Personality type	Understand different personality types at work and exploit best practices with employees for each type	Popular, well known, well researched; many supporting online sites for information and activities; can use the assessement for multiple purposes	Only 16 types and some people could fall into two categories; potential of preconceived notion since it has been around since the early twentieth century	Need to quickly understand the personalities of your team members; get an understanding of how to break up team to most utilize their high-level personality types	http://www.myersbriggs.org/my-mbti-personality-type/mbti-basics/
StandOut	19	Strengths within roles in an organization or team	Learn your team's strengths and your teams, and how to use that knowledge to improve both	Understand 2 roles within strengths and how best to use them with your team individually and in combination from their perspective, not yours	Other than the downloadable report, little support or guidance and few activities are given on the strengths roles once assessment has been taken	Want to onboard several people on a team at once and find out a blended strengths approach in leadership, sales, high-level career advice	https://www.tmbc.com/
What Motivates Me	15	Core motivators	Align interests and motivations with work requirements and needs creating a job focused on motivation	5 identities are easy to understand; recommends uses for an individual's identity, both for themselves and their managers, in easily packaged format	Cost for full online assessment is $40 and is more thorough than the book version; activities and training are additional	Want to compare an individual's strengths or interests with his or her current job and learn how to apply them	http://www.thecultureworks.com

3.4 Real Stories

MBTI: Pulse Check + One-on-Ones = Restarting a Team

I mentioned previously [see Chapter 1] that I had taken over a second team, and that the team had grown to 15 people. Other than an executive assistant and an analyst, I was the most junior person on the entire team in terms of age, with everyone else most likely in their final job. However, many of the team members were relatively new to the company and, in some cases, civilian life. Among our team, I had been at the company the longest, and this proved to be a great asset later in terms of knowing how to get things done within the company (often informally) as well as providing value to the other members on the team in terms of company mentoring.

My immediate task was to assess the other department and figure out where they were in terms of alignment with the GM's objectives and strategic plan. Quickly, it became apparent I had much larger issues to deal with first. Morale among the other department was dismally low. There seemed to be no cohesion or even a sense of team among the team members. The individual team members appeared to lack direction or sense of purpose. I approached the director of HR and requested that an employee engagement survey be conducted so I could get a baseline. On a 5.0 scale (where a 5.0 meant things are superb and at the top of the scale, and the company mean was in the highs 3s), the overall business development (BD) team came in at a 3.1. My current team was at 4.9. This other department was not in a happy, productive place.

I went to my boss, showed him the results of the survey, and proposed to hold a business-development conference. This was a major undertaking as it would incur the cost of flying in the team members who were literally all over the country and world. Fortunately for me, my boss gave me permission.

I worked with my boss and the HR director in coming up with the agenda for the multiday conference. I also asked HR to administer the Myers-Briggs Type Indicator (MBTI) for all of us—a framework that would help each of us understand how we perceived the world and made decisions. This would be for all team members (including myself), whether they already knew their MBTI type or not. I also had HR do a training for us on understanding one's personal MBTI type and, more importantly, how people with different MBTI types do things differently.

Once you understand why and how someone does things, the opportunity opens up to communicate better, make informed compromises, and just generally get along better.

I held one-on-ones with each team member. The individual meetings included a chance to get to know each other on a personal level. The meetings also provided an opportunity to let each person air their grievances in private while also beginning the process to build trust and confidence. We broke bread together for breakfast, lunch, and dinner—by design. I proposed and received acceptance for a team-wide action item/ status tracker on our team's shared drive that would be accessible by all team members (and team members only). I provided an opportunity for each team member to brief the various product managers on where they saw opportunities for each product manager's respective product lines. I also invited our executive assistant and analyst to attend all events. There was one outcome I did not contemplate or foresee. My original team members had many peer-to-peer conversations with the other department team members, letting them know how great things were with the functioning of our original team. The postconference survey seemed to indicate it was a huge success with comments like "I feel I know what's going on better now than the entire time I've been with the company thus far" and "I feel someone is finally listening."

However, having the entire team together for a few days in a connected moment is very different from day-to-day affairs after it's over and everyone is back to their respective areas and responsibilities. I instituted a weekly team meeting where all team members called in. Each team member also got at least five minutes to provide an update on his or her activities as well as to ask any questions so we could share best practices as well as swap stories. I ensured that even our junior team members—our analyst and our executive assistant—were invited to the weekly meetings. I held up my commitment to the BD team members that I would strive to make decisions swiftly, but I also explained what was behind each decision and communicated that during the weekly team meetings we held. Not everyone agreed with every decision, but I think knowing the "why" behind things really went a long way toward acceptance.

—Alex Min

MBTI and Career Anchors in Australia

Whilst working in the Northern Territory (NT) of Australia, I was an operations manager for two separate businesses. In the NT, the workforce is extremely transient, which makes recruiting a fine art and therefore the use of psychometric tools comes in to play. In the other business, a Northern Australian customer service business, I was responsible for recruiting, inducting and training service industry employees.

Within those businesses, I spent most of my time in two sectors—health services for remote communities, and hospitality. I opted to use both MBTI and Career Anchors as the tools that would provide profiles of candidates that would best meet the needs of each community and the various hospitality businesses. These tools, while too detailed for the likelihood of short-term appointments were in fact really useful to gauge what the likely impact these employees would have in each workplace. The assessments provided an overview of preferences for various workplace situations. They also provided the likelihood of how each candidate would deal with problems and scenarios, dealing with aggression—both with colleagues and customers—empathy for clients, career progression, and desired work experiences.

I would strongly encourage other practitioners to utilize these and any other psychometric tools because understanding who you are employing or choosing is critical to both the short-term and medium- to long-term impact those employees have in your workplace.

—Gabriel Oriti, Operations Manager, Bevco Hospitality Group,
Darwin Northern Territory, Australia

Dating and Assessments: How Assessments
Can Help You Find the Real "Talent"

As a human-capital strategy guru, I've learned that talent assessments mitigate my natural biases. For instance, I am extroverted, energetic, and very talkative. I tend to place more value on those traits in candidates if I'm not mindful of the skills, abilities, and characteristics that would be best suited for a particular job profile. An extroverted, energetic and talkative individual may not be well-placed in an individual contributor position that requires minimal interaction with people.

In addition, the interview process is very similar to traditional dating. Although I don't purport to be a relationship expert by any means, I have been on a few dates. Being in the HR profession for more than 20 years, I've also conducted a plethora of job interviews. Dating and interviewing are similar. Generally, my dates and interview candidates were on their best behavior and exhibited wonderful qualities during the introduction and getting-to-know-you period.

However, with a few individuals, sometime later in the relationship (i.e., dating or after the individual was hired) unpleasant traits emerged. If a talent assessment had been required as part of the interview process, these negative behaviors could have been discovered earlier, and most hopefully before the individual was hired. Perhaps using talent assessments for potential dates may improve the matchmaking success statistics!

And finally, I'm also a proponent of using tools, such as StrengthsFinder [now called CliftonStrengths], as a team-building activity. It's an effective way to build awareness, appreciation, and inclusivity of differing strengths and traits among team members.

—Holly Berry, Vice President, Total Beverage Solution

Extroverts and Introverts: Using an Assessment to Lead Differently

Let me share a couple of important facts. The MBTI is a behavior typology assessment based on a dichotomy of four pairs of polarized behaviors (IE, ST, NF, PJ). The MBTI has tremendous application for both personal and organizational needs. I've evaluated nearly a thousand assessments for individuals, couples, groups/teams, and organizations. The results are always the same: those who answer the assessment questions accurately learn how to communicate better with others and ultimately improve organizational efficiencies; improve trust among co-workers, external contacts, and family members; and, ultimately, build better relationships within families, friends, and workplace constituents.

Thousands of books have been written on the benefits of the MBTI, but please allow me to share a few brief snippets on one of the four pairs of MBTI behavior dichotomies that might pique your curiosity.

EI: Extraversion (E) and Introversion (I)

E folks prefer to engage in the outer world while *I* folks prefer to engage introspectively and internally to think through issues. *E* folks think out loud while talking with others, while *I* folks tend to internally process thoughts thoroughly before they share with others, which can lead the *E* folks to believe the *I*s jumped to a conclusion without due consideration.

E/I Dysfunctional Relationship in the Workplace

I completed a workshop with a dysfunctional team where the team leader and a direct report were having workplace conflict. The team leader was an *I* and preferred to keep his office door closed to the team while working on oversight of multiple projects. This quiet setting allowed the *I* to focus on the problem at hand without disruption … a perfect setting for those who build energy in an introspective environment. His direct report project leader, however, was clearly an *E* and often verbally engaged peers and other organizational supervisors to mull over ideas for project development and execution. In fact, several members of the team were clearly extroverted and thus they all functioned well together as they verbalized their daily routines and work-project progress. An *E* team needs engagement to keep its energy up and move forward productively, thus this core team functioned well together.

MISPERCEPTIONS

The *I* leader knew his team worked well together and always generated excellent work that met the needs of the project to the letter. Given specific directions, the *I* team leader had great confidence that, under the *E* project manager's direction, the team would produce quality work. He did not feel compelled to check in daily with the team's progress and knew that if there were any pop-up problems that the project manager could not handle, the project manager would seek his guidance. The *I* leader was comfortable with the process yet was concerned because there seemed to be some negative conversations and destructive grumblings manifesting within the group and he was unsure why.

The *E* project manager was growing more discontent with the *I* team leader's perceived attitude of not caring about the team or project progress. The *I* leader sat behind the closed door and never came out in the workplace to check on the project manager's progress or the quality of his work. The *E* project manager wished the team leader would at least touch base with him at the end of each day. The project manager was growing more concerned about the lack of engagement by the team leader and felt like upper management would never know how hard his team worked or get proper credit for their collective work.

ANALYSIS

Unfortunately, a root issue to misunderstandings between leaders and workers with E/I differences is that the *E* type may mistake the team leader's isolation as an "I don't care about you" attitude and may result in lackluster performance from the *E* workers. If he does not care about excellence, why should I? The cure is quite simple. Once the team members understand the E-I dichotomy, the manager can set a protocol where the *E* team members understand that the *I* manager really has an open-door policy, and when the *E* workers need guidance or input to complete their assignments they merely need to knock on the door and engage the team leader.

There are a variety of strategies to manage E/I differences that can help the team establish a more efficient and productive relationship. For example, the team leader could invite the project manager to visit in his office every other day for a brief update on project progress and the team leader could also invite the project manager to initiate contact with the team leader when issues arise that cannot be handled at the project manager's level.

Alternatively, the *I* team leader might invite the project manager to briefly update him every Friday afternoon on project progress, challenges, and team successes, thus establishing a silent open-door policy. Finally, the team leader should publicly acknowledge the overall team's successes with an additional kind word acknowledging the project manager's role in the team's work product. The key to every intervention is to not allow assumptions, inferences, and presumptions to go without validation or one risks maturing manifestations of negative emotions and destructive conflict outcomes within any team dynamic.

—Dr. Gary Boettcher, Founder, Conflict Management Strategies Inc,
Master Myers-Briggs practitioner

Using the Talent Engagement Zone to Self-analyze Your Leadership

The Talent Engagement Assessment is pretty spot on. I fell into the Yellow category. The questions asked made me realize I have to seriously consider my position because I don't feel that I am using all my talents or reaching my potential.

—Dana Sadowsky, Member Services, Wicklander-Zulawski and Associates

StrengthsFinder as More Than Just an Assessment

As a young woman who works in higher education, I have a unique opportunity to connect with college students in ways their professors may never have. I see two roles in higher education. The academic professors build students' confidence in their knowledge about information. My role as an assistant director in the college's leadership development program allows me to help students build confidence in their innate talents and in themselves.

I've been employed by the same institution since the inception of my professional career. While interviewing for the position, I remember it was suggested that I complete the StrengthsFinder (now known as CliftonStrengths) Assessment. It was my first interaction with the assessment and the accompanying information. When hired, I remember being uneasy about introducing my student staff to the concept; my ability to explain how beneficial each talent theme is to a team was severely underdeveloped.

It was in my second year as a residential education coordinator that my inadequate skill in clearly expressing the assets within each person met an insecure student staff member. The tears she cried that day left a permanent stain on the T-shirt of my mind. In the months that followed, I coddled her instead of helping her work through the struggles she had with using her skills and knowledge within a team.

Instead of helping her develop herself and getting her to a level of comfort with her talents, I pushed her to perform in ways that benefitted the reputation of the staff, but not the relationships among the staff. When I left the staff midyear for a new position, I remember learning that her management of her relationship with other staff members plummeted. This let me know that I did nothing to fortify her confidence in the positive power that comes from her talents. I fortified her confidence in the shadow sides of her talent themes. As a result, she became the most self-serving yet most successful person on the staff, which gave her a false sense of accomplishment.

I was determined not to repeat that mistake. Fast forward four years and I am now a Gallup-Certified Strengths Coach in addition to my current role with the university.

Having learned the foundations of coaching and best practices of facilitating discussions around the assessment results, I knew exactly how to approach talent-based discussions.

I currently work with a student who I'll call Mariah. Mariah has an energy that is unmatched. However, her fast-paced style of communication, her high level of excitability, and her desire to help others are often misinterpreted as pushy, talkative, and annoying. Mariah has bumped her head a few times while completing tasks on behalf of our office, which has slightly tarnished her reputation in the eyes of professional staff. In an effort to redirect her energy, we agreed to a coaching session.

In our session, we determined that her major issue was not creating enough time in her schedule to prepare for upcoming tasks and assignments, which is why she appeared rushed. Despite that projection, she and I discussed how using her dominant talent themes could combat her hurried nature. One major action-based solution we developed for her performance was matching her talents to specific tasks that would allow her to sharpen her talents toward strengths.

—*Nadia Campbell, Assistant Director, Leadership Development*

SECTION 3

Days 26–50: Starting, Resisting, and Becoming "Who"

CHAPTER 4

The Results Are In!
What to Do with Them?
(Analyzing Initial Results)

4.1 The SBSG Story

Elizabeth looks down at her paper, crosses out what she just wrote, and looks up at the monitor screen again. The data collection, the results of a combination of interviews of the 10 team members—across two different teams—and a short assessment were listed in a spreadsheet patchwork of rows and boxes. She feels a headache growing the more she looks at the figures boxes.

"So, what's the next logical step?" Avery asks brightly as she comes in the room, loaded down with a laptop, coffee (for Elizabeth), and a diet soda (for herself). Avery is an outside consultant that SBSG brought in for operational and developmental project direction. She has a perky personality and energy that never seem to stop. Elizabeth grumbles over Avery's "logical" mentality—easy for her to say. She takes a long sip of coffee in her favorite silver cup.

"Uh ... group the data?" Elizabeth responds, only partially ironically.

"Excellent," Avery bubbles, "and how should we group them?"

Elizabeth takes a deep breath and another long sip from her coffee. She guesses that "we group them the way that Avery tells me to" is not the answer that Avery is looking for in this riddle of data in front of her. She *is* interested—she knows the results she is working toward and wants to get there—she just may need some more coffee first.

4.2 The Nuts and Bolts

There are two parts to talent engagement optimization (TEO)—talent engagement (TE) and optimization (O). If you are comfortable working with people and enjoy motivating, developing, and helping others get to the next level—TE is your world. However, if you live for numbers and dream up complicated PivotTable VLOOKUP functions in Excel—the optimization side of this equation is for you.

At this point, you're several weeks into the TEO project, and you have gathered data—in some form or fashion—via assessment, interviews, or other methods. You have a lot of data, probably spread around many areas: in a Word document here, in an e-mail there, maybe even on a few scraps of paper. It's now time to put all of that together to understand what you have, find the trends, and make use of it to move forward on fully engaging the talent you have in your organization.

Getting Started: Focusing on the Data in Your Assessment

Let's assume that you have already collected some data—either quantitative (numeric in some way) or qualitative (primarily words, such as interviews). If you've performed assessments, they can be considered both quantitative (for example, how many people received "relator" as a strength?) and qualitative (such as we have a lot of people in the "motivating others" category—what does that mean?).

How much data do you need to have at this point? That's a good question, but you don't need to have a finite answer (or a tremendous amount of data). Think about your baseline—your starting point (see Chapter 1.3, "Activities and Application"). You will need data to support the transition from that benchmark you created—to make it relevant.

What if you have 50 employees? Interviewing 10 percent of the workforce is only five people and is not much of a sample size, but you may be able to conduct a combination of assessments and short interviews to obtain enough data. Have a CEO or leader who needs lots of numbers? You will probably have to gather a bit more data to satisfy their desire for the facts through data.

Briefly, list the benchmarks that you decide in the Introduction ("The Best Ways to Succeed with This Book") and the criteria for success (for example, improve this metric by 10 percent, increase engagement survey results by 15 percent over last year).

_____

_____

_____

_____

_____

_____

_____

_____

The goal of reading the results from the assessments you conduct is to make sense of a mountain of data. Whether the activity is called "research" or "trend analysis," you are trying to parse the results and understand the information in front of you.

Trend analysis is the ability to take somewhat unrelated data and find the ways they are actually related—in a way that is important to you, your research, and your ultimate goals. In true academic research, most results are unknown. Hence, we develop hypotheses to direct our research toward an outcome.

Likewise, you don't actually know the results until you analyze the data, but you do know what you'd like them to look like. You want the results to offer a clear outcome on whether or not we're on the right path to developing a more productive organization.

You want to have a more engaged workforce. You'd like to streamline your people processes or give people more time back in their day. All of these things are the goals, and—as in academic research—you focus on these goals, your "research question," when digging into the data. Focus on the goal, what you're trying to resolve, and it will help you align your benchmark metrics to your final (successful!) results.

I had to learn this process the hard way. When I first started researching, I was constantly all over the place until I finally found a trick that worked—writing the research question on an index card and putting it eye level at my desk.

Therefore, any time I was thinking or was stuck, I would lean back in my chair and automatically see this index card telling me exactly what my focus was. It's always important to have a goal in mind—something to center your efforts around. If I encountered information that didn't relate, I moved on. I didn't get rid of it, but I put it in a parking lot for potential use later.

Finding the Trends

Now let's explore how we can use both quantitative and qualitative data to identify trends in our research results.

QUANTITATIVE

With quantitative data, you are looking for numbers. Perhaps an example here would help to explain the connection for the numbers you are searching. I once researched people who had "promoted themselves to customer," or quit their job (Lesko 2016a). They shared their opinions about why they left.

My survey asked, "Think about the reason(s) you left your company. What percent of your reasons for leaving was due to the following? (Please make sure they add up to 100.)"

Respondents could choose from several options stating why they might have left (as well as a fill-in-the-blank "other" option). The survey software exported the results—raw data—into an Excel spreadsheet. Raw data haven't been analyzed or formatted—like milk that has just come out of a cow, nothing has been added or changed.

My main assessment question was "What are the main reasons people would voluntarily choose to leave a company?" I looked at each of the columns of data to find out how many people decided that a certain item, such as "company culture," affected their reason to leave.

Take a look at Table 4.1. Let's say that out of 200 respondents, 75 considered company culture to be at least one of the reasons for leaving; that's 37.5 percent (75/200). If I worked at a company that prided itself on having a strong culture, I would share this data point with the leadership team.

The same ideas apply to other assessments you might use, such as CliftonStrengths (formerly known as StrengthsFinder) or What Motivates Me. From your assessment, you have a list of responses, which you can break out separately into groups to understand:

Individuals/Employees

- How many people have strengths in verbal communication? How many have our key cultural skill (customer service, for instance)?
- What percentage of the people surveyed have this concern or strength? Is this percentage acceptable? Should that percentage be higher? Lower? If so, how will we achieve our desired goals? (See Chapter 5, "Building the Action Plan," for more details, but make sure to write your question down now!)
- How many individuals feel they are using their strengths or having their concerns addressed?

Teams/Organization

- What are your metrics of success (benchmark/results)? How many people agreed they are prepared to support the key metric of success such as leadership trust or engagement at work?
- Which measurements could explain the areas that your company is having problems in or would like to improve, such as not enough staff to get job done or working too many hours?
- How can we use the information provided from the assessments to create a conducive work environment?

QUALITATIVE

If "quantitative" or "quant" for short is looking at data for the *numbers*, then "qualitative" or "qual" is looking at the data for the *words*! Qualitative data can be somewhat more cumbersome than its quantitative brother—whereas quantitative data are black-and-white numbers (it either is 22 or it's not), qualitative data tends to be relative, in the eye of the beholder.

Let's assume you have interviewed five existing employees as part of your TEO assessment. You took notes, or, if you were really motivated, you recorded the interviews and documented every word. That is the best way to interview, but for us practitioners out there, it's sometimes hard to get to that level of thoroughness!

TABLE 4.1. Excerpt of Raw Data from "I Didn't Quit My Job, I Fired My Company"

LACK OF ADVANCEMENT	SENIOR MANAGEMENT	MY DIRECT MANAGER	UNSATISFIED WITH BENEFITS/ PAY	DIDN'T FEEL CONNECTED TO ORGANIZATION	WORK/LIFE BALANCE	COMPANY CULTURE	WORK ENVIRONMENT	OTHER
50	10	0	30	10	0	0	0	0
70	10	0	10	0	0	0	0	10
20	0	60	0	0	0	0	0	20
0	20	60	0	0	0	10	10	0
20	50	10	20	0	0	0	0	0
0	0	50	0	0	50	0	0	0
0	0	50	20	0	0	10	20	0

Now let's organize our notes so that we can analyze our findings and identify any trends:

How to Turn Words from an Assessment into Data You Can Use

1. *Gather all your notes.* Put them in one location.
2. *Organize your notes.* Use your preferred method for organizing your thoughts and work. For me, this is in Excel.
3. *Transfer your notes.* Enter text into columns (for example, in a spreadsheet or table) with labels such as these:
   - Name
   - Position
   - Department/Team (if important)
   - Comment
   - Trend

   For an example of a quantitative analysis, see Table 4.2 on page 65.
4. *Insert trends in one column.* Enter a summary word or two (for example, "unengaged" or "wants more leadership"). To recognize possible trends in the interview responses, and therefore in the workplace itself, try to use the same term or phrase to summarize similar responses from your notes. This approach will let you easily focus on problem areas and other issues to address. What do people say a lot? By categorizing simple words, you can identify the high-level opportunities—or "low-hanging fruit."

You Don't Judge a Book by Its Cover—So Don't Assume Your Data Are Perfect, Either

Ask any analyst that does this work full time for one of their top concerns, and you'll hear that it is having incorrect data, or improperly analyzed data. Your output is as good as your input—but what do you do with the information when you're reviewing it? To help you out, take a look at the next sections for some of the most commonly seen pitfalls to look out for when analyzing your data.

Trust but verify

Caution: the advice I'm about to give you is actually twofold. It's information that you can use here, in analyzing data, but it also secretly serves another purpose—and that is how to be a good leader. Throughout the book, you may have realized that leadership is a theme. Here is another one of those "crucible" moments. If you have never heard of the *Crucibles of Leadership,* I highly recommend the read. You may have some of your own.

The concept of "trust but verify" is true for your data, your team, and your boss. You have the information, but is it right? Does it represent the actual situation, or what you want it to represent (these two are not always the same)? In the academic world, this problem (not verifying the data, or going with the wrong data) has terminated careers and ended jobs.

To shed light on the importance of accurate data, let's take an extreme case. Imagine if a surgeon was underreporting how long a patient was using a heart-lung bypass machine while in surgery. That was the case of surgeon Ian Wilson from the Queen Elizabeth Hospital. Dozens of patients were impacted by needlessly corrupted data (Smith and Sawer 2014). To relate that story to the importance of verification, inaccurate data can lead to the wrong diagnoses and focuses of an organization.

Here's a checklist to help you verify your data:

1. *Determine the type of information you are verifying and the number of people in your assessment.*
   - What type of assessment are you using? Are you focusing on engagement? Strengths? Leadership?
   - What's the total number of people being assessed (N)? If you interviewed 10 people out of 50 (20 percent), you have a good frame of reference, but if you interviewed 10 out of 10,000, then you interviewed only 0.1 percent. Do you want to change the entire organization based on those 10 people's interviews? Probably not.
   - How does this information affect success in the program?
2. *Take a step back.* Sometimes immersing yourself in the data can cause implicit bias. Wait an hour or two or even a day. Do the data make sense?
3. *Confirm as accurate.* Take a look one more time—is this the information you wanted to see? Or does it show something else that you didn't expect or may not way to see? How do you use it?
4. *Don't be afraid to ask questions if someone else did the assessment.* Asking questions will help you understand the person's research method. Sample questions to ask include the following:
   - How did you obtain these data?
   - Can you walk me through one of the data collections you did?
5. *Check the results.* Are you ready to take a stand on what the data are telling you? If so, proceed to the next section.

GET FEEDBACK—LOTS OF IT

Feedback can be the best form of flattery. However, whether you're starting out as a leader or crossing the 20-year mark, it's never easy to receive critical feedback. Sure, it may improve your performance, but you have to hear how you weren't as great as you thought you were. Thicken your skin and keep listening.

Receiving critical feedback as a leader or in your data is never easy. Once you've analyzed the results and understand where your trends are going, or what the interviews are telling you, ask a few people that you believe will give you honest feedback. These could be people whom you interviewed or surveyed, or an advisor or peer whose feedback you value! Ask them, "Do these results make sense to you?" If you conclude that 75 percent of employees surveyed want to leave early on Thursdays for a 10 percent pay cut, you had better be confident that's the case before recommending the change to finance!

Obtaining feedback is also a part of verifying data. Ask your assessment participants to review the results to ensure you've correctly interpreted their input. At the end of the day, the impact of the feedback will directly affect their work life.

Feedback is also a crucial part of testing, learning, and refining. Your output will not determine the optimal method of increasing performance and productivity in one shot. Implementing change will be an iterative process of enhancing and releasing. To reach that optimal point, you'll need to receive feedback from the people actually affected by the change to determine the best strategy going forward.

USING YOUR COUP D'OEIL

While reading for a course I am taking, I came across a term that gave me pause—*coup d'oeil* (pronounced "coo dwell"). Literally translated from French, it means "stroke of the eye" or, in general, a glance or a look.

However, theorists over the centuries have taken the term further and used it to describe a strategy or ability to see things at a glance.

Indeed, after reading more about the term, I would even sum it up more simply—a *coup d'oeil* is a summary glance in which meaning is drawn. In one look, you can see beyond what's there. Read between the lines. See things that others don't.

You may find yourself scratching your head a bit, wondering how a summary glance could help with people analysis. This chapter is aimed at helping you *break out* of your current state and help you find new information in data that you already have. After you assess or interview your team members, they will remain the same people. But *you* now have the chance to look at them differently, perhaps with a perspective you haven't had before. So, review your notes. You may find a new perspective you didn't see earlier but had been there all along.

So … how do you best use your *coup d'oeil*? I'll ask you to give it some thought as you go through the ways you can improve your leadership by strengthening your *coup d'oeil* skills:

- You only get a first chance to make a first impression. Other people take an average of seven seconds to figure out who you are, or will be, to them (Goman 2001). You do the same thing. What do you learn from that glance? Their attitude or personality? Do they smile or make eye contact? Be aware when meeting people and cultivating and growing relationships that a *coup d'oeil*, or summary glance, means you too are making these snap judgments without even thinking about them. Be cognizant of the fact that these judgments of others may not always be right and that your perceptions may be directed more by your own experiences or what's happening in your life. These perceptions could give your *coup d'oeil* a foggy perspective. Make sure to clear the lenses off so that you're seeing what's really around you clearly.

- Knowledge is power. The more you learn or know about a situation, the more you can recognize patterns based on your experience and be prepared for the unknown. Think of your local firefighters. They practice their drills over and over again, responding in different ways to different problems—sometimes even with different equipment—so that they'll be prepared to respond appropriately to multiple situations. The more experienced you are, the better you're able to use your *coup d'oeil* skill to accurately recognize situations and respond accordingly. For example, you may try a new way to talk to a difficult employee or to work with a senior manager who seems distant. Maybe the solution to your problem lies in a strategy that worked for another department or team. What can you prepare ahead of time that will help you recognize new or challenging situations faster and more accurately?

- Through experience, you can increase your skill in using *coup d'oeil*. Yes, people are born with talents. Some are better singers, some can make a mean apple pie without looking at a recipe, and others are natural leaders. Just as you are developing your leadership of employees, peers, and others, you can sharpen your insight through experience, experimentation, and practice. Oh, and not giving up. You will most likely grasp failure once or twice—but your *coup d'oeil* strengthens every time you use it. (Lesko 2016b)

4.3 Activities and Application

The following is an example of qualitative analysis (see Lesko 2016a). I performed the interviews and assigned each person an anonymous code name in the first column. There was no need to record a department or company name, so I left that information out of the table. The second column lists the comments that I noted from the interviews (in this case, they were comments I had jotted down in a Word document). I listed the trends in the final column.

- Here's a key to deciphering the codes in the table:
  - NM = new manager
  - CA = career anchor; LS, CH, TF, GM, SV = types of career anchors (LS = lifestyle, CH = pure challenge, TF = technical/functional, GM = general managerial, SV = service/dedication to a cause)
  - WE = work engagement
- Take a look at the trends—which patterns, words, and occurences do you see?
- Using initials or abbreviations, as seen in this table, can save time, but if you need to share the data in this form, you may want to use complete phrases and terms.

4.4 Real Stories

Quantitative Analysis to Help Make Leadership Decisions

All teams are made up of a variety of talents. Each person on the team is unique and brings a different talent to the team. When I was appointed vice chancellor of academic affairs at a community college, I was given the opportunity to build my team from scratch.

I used a profile instrument that accessed each candidate's thinking and behavior attributes and I built my team ensuring that all parts of the brain were represented on the team. The four attributes were analytical, structural, social, and conceptional. With

TABLE 4.2.   Qualitative Data—Output Example

NAME	COMMENTS	TREND
LS11	Comment [APL1]: Expecting TF or GM for CA	NM is partial the CA
TF40	Comment [APL1]: Feeling like don't closely identify this—(perhaps feelings of other CA she wants more?)	NM is partial the CA
CH49	Comment [APL1]: Supports the CA assigned	NM is the CA
CH49	Comment [APL10]: By doing CA, has achieved her goal	CA is important in career
LS11	Comment [APL11]: Disappointing to have seniority only to lose it at another company, lower WE	LS needs control, lower WE
SV53	Comment [APL12]: CA background—influence by mom to become nurse, purpose behind helping SV	SV has background in CA
LS11	Comment [APL12]: Senior people/managers leave company for better companies, not better roles, feeling lower WE	Lack of control, lower WE
LS44	Comment [APL13]: Memo: Average WE driven by a positive (new area, learning) and negative (working more hours)—can there be a scale in here somewhere compared to others?	Memo
SV53	Comment [APL13]: Memo: She is a young manager, wants to grow to help in bigger areas—is there a connection here? Those that are managers tend to want more in their CA than those that don't?	NM want more in their CA than those that don't?
LS11	Comment [APL14]: Feeling only way to be noticed by manager is by doing something bad, lowering WE	LS needs support, lower WE
LS44	Comment [APL15]: Memo: Feels has the ability to control his LS WE. This exactly correlates with his numbers that he gets it in his job and he gets as much as he wants	LS needs control, higher WE

* In this example, career anchors and work engagement numbers were based on the research, and shared here only as a reference. For more information on Career Anchors or Work Engagment, take a look at the References Section.

all four attributes represented, I had the right team with the right talents and was able to become very successful as a team. Most people hire others who are like them since that is what they are comfortable with. The challenge is to hire those who are different than you to form the best team.

—Marilyn Faulkenburg, professor, Sullivan University

It's the Soft Stuff: Breaking Down the Hard Decisions of Quantity versus Quality in Projects

How to Choose a Project?

In selecting a project there are many data variables that come into play and the data generally falls into two categories, quantitative and qualitative data. In project selection, a project should be based on how the initiative will align with the organizational strategic objectives. With that said, all data including return on investments, profits, environmental enhancements, or a company's competitive advantage should be researched and reviewed before proceeding. A clearly defined outline of what is important to an organization should be a baseline in determining project selections.

QUALITATIVE VERSUS QUANTITATIVE DATA?

First, what is the difference between qualitative or quantitative data? At first glance, these two words may seem very similar, yet their meanings are entirely different and should be carefully considered in selecting projects.

Which is better to use, qualitative or quantitative data? The answer is, it depends. Determining which is the best data really depends on the capacity available for data research. Qualitative data generally measures attributes and characteristics. This is where your data has more feeling and is expressed in a more subjective manner. Whereas, quantitative data is based on raw facts and bottom-line results. This is a more concise depiction of evidence-based data with structured facts.

MY PERSONAL TAKE?

As an HR practitioner, I have found that deployment of both quantitative and qualitative data is key in making sound business decisions. Objective decisions rely on data which is derived from the compilation of reports, surveys, reviews, and questionnaires. Quantitative data is your concrete evidence. Quantitative data gives a verified baseline and supports why a project or task should be selected. It is equally important to access the qualitative data that speaks to the attributes or characteristics that give answers to the "why" of a project. Qualitative data offers more feeling; it is more subjective and empathetic. Qualitative data speaks to the human side of things.

Personally, my background in recruitment required utilization of quantitative and qualitative data in the selection process of employees. The quantitative data that I used came from the job description that I would receive from the hiring manager. The job description was the outlined skills required to be successful in the open role. Unfortunately, through many trial and errors, I found that utilizing quantitative data alone did not prove to be 100 percent successful.

A job description (quantitative data) alone does not fulfill a position successfully. It was only when I combined the qualitative data, the desired attributes of the potential hire, and the knowledge of the characteristics of the department with the quantitative data (job description) that I began to have a winning combination. The job description plus the soft skill requirements (qualitative data) of the candidate and the characteristics of the department is what fully completes a successful match. Therefore, the utilization of both quantitative and qualitative data is for well-informed decision-making.

WHAT IS THE BOTTOM LINE?

Exactly, this is the question that should be asked in every project-selection process. What is the bottom line? The bottom line is what drives our organizations. Is our final result or outcome of a project aligned with our organizational strategic objectives? Considering both qualitative and quantitative data in project selection ensures that the bottom-line results will be achieved.

—*Takisha B. Clyburn, PMP, CSSGB, CTS*

CHAPTER 5

Building the Action Plan. Caution, Construction Zone Ahead!

5.1 The SBSG Story

Elizabeth blinks. It's finished.

It took the better part of a day (and about two and a half full pots of coffee), but the initial analysis is done. The majority of the results don't surprise her (which is good—she would be concerned if the results were a surprise!), but still, a good 30 percent or so of the results is unexpected.

That unexpected part is the icing on the cake to Elizabeth. She knows she wants to increase productivity by 10 percent as a TEO goal in each department that was part of the project, and she has ideas of how to do it. But some of these employee suggestions, such as cross-training outside the department—way outside the department (who would have thought someone in operations would want to learn marketing?)—were completely unexpected.

Could the TEO goal be accomplished? Could it be implemented at SBSG?

And if so, how could accomplishing the TEO goal be done? What steps would she and the organization need to take—and in what order? How long would accomplishing the TEO goal take?

She knows the goal—where she wants to end up. She knows the data and where she and her team are. Now she has to figure out how to reach the destination.

She needs an action plan.

5.2 The Nuts and Bolts

Take action , but first read this. If you are a person of action, there is a very good possibility that you have skipped the first four chapters and the introduction (let alone the table of contents!) and started here. You already know what's going on—you have obtained leadership support, done your assessment, and analyzed your data for trends. Now, you just need to figure out how to carry out your TEO plan.

I am blessed (or cursed, as some would say) with the ability to shoot straight to the problem—go to where the solution is—and make things happen. I may not have the problem solved, but we'll figure out the details on the way, right?

However, we are dealing *with other people* here, so it may be worth your time to take a few steps before you start running (or at least do a few warm-ups before the run!).

The next section will help you get there. I've said it before: my military ways have created a love for checklists. If you are one that does not like form and order, then think of it as following a recipe in your favorite cookbook. How do you prepare for cooking the recipe for that cake or casserole? You (typically) get the ingredients out before starting the recipe for two reasons:

- To confirm you aren't out of anything.
- To have the ingredients at your fingertips when you start cooking.

It's a good plan of action to have your ingredients (i.e., inputs) ready for building your action plan. Let's see where we stand, and get ready to get cooking!

Getting the Ingredients Ready for the Recipe

You have three main ingredients that you have already worked on, measured, and reviewed. Let's get them out and see where we are. Review the ingredients below and make sure you have them all.

Pre–Action Plan Ingredient Checklist

1. ____ Get on the Train—Buy-In (Chapter 1)
2. ____ What Cards Are in Your Hand?—Choosing the Assessment (Chapter 3)
3. ____ The Results Are In!—Understanding the Analysis (Chapter 4)

SECURE BUY-IN FROM STAKEHOLDERS

Chapter 1 explains the importance of making sure your company, leadership team, and executives (basically anyone who would be important in supporting your action plan) buy in to the idea and concept of improving their team through talent engagement. The idea is to ensure that everyone is aligned on the vision and goals—and the plan of action to accomplish them.

Review the following items to ensure success in this area:

1. *Perform a gap analysis.* Do you have a thorough understanding of where your organization or team is now and where you want to go? What is the starting point? Where is the end state? How did you analyze those differences?

_____

_____

_____

_____

_____

_____

_____

_____

2. *Define success.* What does success look like for this project?

_____

_____

_____

_____

_____

_____

_____

3. *Identify the goal.* There may be more than one goal for the project. It may be different than what you have defined for success. How do you know you have obtained
the goal? What metrics will change/improve/decrease?

_____

_____

_____

_____

_____

_____

_____

4. *Obtain executive buy-in.* Do you have it? Who supports the project? Who still needs
to be convinced? What level of engagement do they want to have with the project? You may need to be prepared to answer the question: what will be expected of
executives in the future? (See Chapter 6 for additional suggestions.)

_____

_____

_____

_____

_____

_____

CHOOSE THE INSTRUMENT

The purpose of Chapter 3 is to learn, assess, and decide on the best way to gather information about the strengths and talents of your team. A variety of choices, methods, and timing is discussed.

Review the following items to ensure success in this area:

1. *Method for information.* What method did you choose to obtain more information about your team (e.g., assessment, interviews)? Why?

_____

_____

_____

_____

_____

_____

_____

2. *Reasons for Specific Instrument Choice.* What are the three key reasons for choosing the instrument or methods that you did? What are its strengths? What are its disadvantages? How will you overcome the disadvantages (if necessary)?

_____

_____

_____

_____

_____

_____

_____

_____

_____

3. *Instrument Impact to Goals.* How does the instrument or method correlate to the goals and the success of the project as deemed in the previous section?

_____

_____

_____

_____

_____

_____

_____

_____

_____

UNDERSTAND THE ANALYSIS

The purpose of Chapter 4 is to evaluate the results of the data in the completed assessment. The chapter presents different methods, focusing on numbers (quantitative) or words (qualitative), and gives examples of their uses.

Review the following items to ensure success in this area:

1. *High-level results.* What are the high-level results obtained from your assessment that you can quickly explain to your executives (if needed)?

_____

_____

_____

_____

_____

_____

_____

_____

_____

2. *Trending results and outcomes.* What key trends did you see from the results? (They may or may not be part of the high-level results in the previous question.)

_____

_____

_____

_____

_____

_____

_____

_____

_____

3. *Feedback from trends.* Upon completing your analysis, with whom have you discussed your results to obtain feedback? What feedback was given? Did your analysis make sense to the people you spoke with? Did the trends connect with the information they see or perceive? If not, how did you address the trends?

_____

_____

_____

_____

_____

_____

_____

_____

_____

_____

Lights, Camera, Action Plan!

Let's talk a little about what action plans generally look like. An *action plan* is generally a list of items set in a certain order for the purpose of accomplishing a certain goal or goals. An action plan can vary from company to company and from individual to individual. Elon Musk, for example, had a five-line action plan that seemed to work for him (Musk 2006):

1. Build a sports car.
2. Use the money from the sales of the sports car to build an affordable car.
3. Use *that* money (from the affordable car) to build an even more affordable car.
4. While doing the above, also provide zero-emission electric power generation options.
5. Don't tell anyone.

However, what works for one company, culture, and individual may not work for another. Others may require more detail. For example, a government agency may have a project plan requiring a comprehensive design to manage an experienced employee base of over two thousand individuals versus a startup with 10 employees that makes (and changes) a plan almost daily.

Perhaps your organization requires a happy medium between the two. The general idea is that your action plan should be the outcome of your previous steps—which include gathering and analyzing your data and identifying your team's individual strengths. As long as your action plan maintains the core components mentioned in the previous chapters, you should have a strong foundation on which you can continue to build and develop.

Like an architect who looks at an empty lot and envisions a building to develop, you have just as many ways to develop your action plan. I tend to start with the goal (build the house) and then develop the outline (framing) and timeline (dates for completing each stage). From there, I fill in the details (the important stuff—like the plumbing, electricity, and drywall).

The next pages address a few ways you can design your action plan in a way that works for you, your team, and your organization. What will your building look like? That's up to you.

Parts of an Action Plan

An *action plan* is defined by the Google dictionary as a "proposed strategy or course of action." To me, whenever I see the word "strategy" in a definition, I believe there are a number of different methods to solve the problem. Strategy allows for flexibility. Your action plan should be flexible, but with a specific purpose or goal in mind.

A simple action plan can be a single table or spreadsheet for *each* of the goals you want to accomplish—and then columns to show the results, effects, tasks, and action to complete. Potential columns could be

- Goal (objective).
- Activities (tasks)—specifically what needs to be done.
- Location (where)—if specific location is important.
- Metrics addressing—metric to be measured.
- Success criteria—knowing when this task/goal is successful.
- Timing (deadline)—task completion date.
- Resources (people)—who is needed to complete the task.
- Resources (material)—what is needed to complete the task.
- Potential constraints—obstacles to finishing the task by the deadline.
- Priority level (importance level)—ordered by necessity or impact, based on timing or otherwise, to give weight to the task's importance.
- Impact (cost/savings)—in dollars, hours, or other return on investment (ROI) areas that could help define the priority for resources or help explain savings of project.
- Impact (people)—who will be affected during this task (for example, because of a system upgrade, email will be down for twenty-four hours for the entire department, or an entire team will not be working because of needed training that will last for two hours).
- Marketing (strategy)—how the plan will be rolled out.

TABLE 5.1.   Example Goal to Action Planning Sheet

GOAL	TASK/ACTIVITY	TIMING	METRICS ADDRESSING	SUCCESS CRITERIA	RESOURCES—PEOPLE
Increasing employee productivity	Engage at least one specific strength	By end of 100 days	Employee productivity/capacity	All 10 employees on team will be using one strength outside of job description	All people on team + manager—2x/month for one hour each

Questions to Ask Yourself When Building Your Action Plan

What do you want to do in your action plan?

_____

_____

_____

_____

_____

What is your timing? Your constraints?

_____

_____

_____

_____

_____

Do you have a limitation in hours, dollars, other? Do you have to show results within a specific time frame? What is the deadline?

_____

_____

_____

_____

_____

_____

How many people are involved? The greater the number, the longer you want to provide timeline support.

_____

_____

_____

_____

_____

_____

Additional examples of action plan inputs can be found in Part 3 of this chapter.

Do You Know How to Celebrate Your Birthday?

When you're building the action plan, you may find yourself a little disheartened, thinking "there's no way the team and the executives will buy in; the timing won't work; it's too much work." Persistence is key here, and even more important are the celebrations that you build into your action plan. Make sure to add in a few celebrations to your action plan and its milestones.

Each year, we celebrate the passing of one more year. We've lived 525,600 minutes (thanks to the musical *Rent* and the song of the same name), eaten our lunch, worked, had some fun, worked some more, thought about vacation, and experienced a few other things.

What about the other things? The peaks and the valleys, the highs and the lows? The breakups and the successes, the "wow" moments and the "oh no!" moments?

This leads me to the question, Do you know how to celebrate your employee's "birthdays"?

I'm not just talking about cake, flowers, or maybe a day off if you're a really nice boss. I'm talking about the celebration part. The "thank you for doing a great job" part. The "today, you should be celebrated because you did this" part. The "I don't even know what kind of sacrifice you made to get this done, but I recognize it, and I thank you for it." Get my drift?

Celebrate successes. Make employees feel special. Offer recognition to individuals and teams. Even little baby successes—like learning to complete that first PowerPoint presentation without correction by the VP—that may not seem like much to you. Thank your people. Thanking them is the basis of countering two (anonymity and immeasurability) of the three (irrelevance is the third) pillars of having a miserable job (Lencioni 2007).

And you've probably already seen this coming … why stop at birthdays?

For the people who work for you, day in and day out, who get it done every day—celebrate successes. Did your team finish a project that was 90 percent great but 10 percent needing improvement? Do not focus only on the improvements (and yes, honestly, I still struggle with this!). Sing "Happy Birthday" to those who made it great (that is, make them feel special and appreciated) and then the next day (when it's not their "birthday"), tackle the 10 percent and raise the mark.

Try it. It won't hurt. It may feel a little funny at first, but your people will like it. (*Adapted from Lesko 2016.*)

5.3 Activities and Application

Action Plan Example Steps

Part 5.2 gave you the high-level approach as well as a few specific examples of building the action plan. This section will go more into specific uses, examples, and tactical moves you can do to not only build your action plan but reinforce it so that it is easier to manage and will help you relate the information more effectively in the transition.

One of the challenges that implementers of projects tend to have is that they can't see the forest for the trees, meaning they are so focused on the prize or the goal—how they will help everyone or save the world—they lose sight of other perspectives.

This section will share insight on a few out-of-the box approaches that several industries have used successfully. Try one or add it to a step in your action plan.

Some of the approaches, such as in those referencing strengths, could use the information provided in an assessment that your team took. In these cases, the exercises and tasks are referenced as starting points. You would then develop your plan based on the unique results for your team. (See Figure 5.1 for a suggested planning outline.)

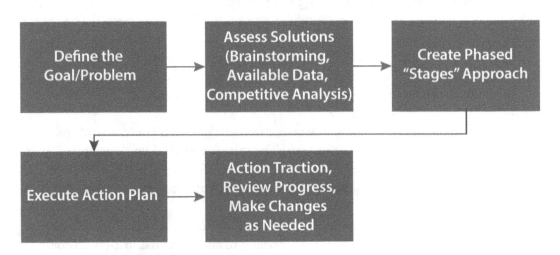

FIGURE 5.1. Suggested Planning Outline

Action Plan—Suggested Approaches

STREAMLINING A "DIRTY" PROCESS

Goal: Reduce time and steps in a repeated process.

Type: Quantitative

Ease of use: Moderate difficulty

Explanation: Understand the problem. For those not familiar with traditional streamlining approaches found in operations, this activity may require some research. Take a few minutes to look up the following: You would start by learning where the largest problems are using a tool such as a Pareto chart and then work to reduce steps and eliminate as many of the seven types of waste in your process. If the process takes 60 minutes (on average) to complete, what are the three to five tasks that take the majority of that time? Focus on these.

- **Waste.** Once you understand where the waste in the system is, see if you can Pareto (eliminate or reduce) those systems as well—get the waste out!
- **Putting it all together.** Once you've found the biggest time issues and waste concerns in the system, find ways to eliminate them. Brainstorm, develop ideas, discard them, ask for feedback, and build new processes.
- **Buy-in.** Every problem's solution needs people to support it. Get the people closest to the problem to support the new system.

Notes:

_____

_____

_____

_____

_____

_____

_____

_____

_____

_____

TRACKING THE METRICS—BUILDING A DASHBOARD

Goal: Have pertinent, relevant information at your fingertips when you need it.

Type: Quantitative

Ease of use: High difficulty

Explanation: Perhaps your team members have realized they are unproductive because they don't know how well they are doing something. I have also seen several business that did not measure their processes so the leaders accepted whatever length of time their employees took to finish a job. Your team members understanding the "what" and "how" of your action plan is important, but understanding how their key metrics relate to our goals and how we planned to obtain them is even more important.

- **Find the metrics.** Where will the information come from? What numbers are needed? Where is the source?
- **Build a dashboard.** Do you have a dashboard already created or do you need to build it? A dashboard is a central place for a team, department, or organization to reference how they are using metrics at any given time. Many dashboards already exist—some companies already have them built into their business's current software package—they just don't know it. If you think you have it, ask the software team. If you don't, you can create it with something as simple as Excel.
- **Make it easy to understand.** Don't make the dashboard so complicated that you are the only one who can operate it.
- **Make it easily repeatable.** How does the data get into the dashboard? Is it simply linking two Excel sheets? Uploading a file? Updating or uploading to a dashboard should take no more than 30 seconds.
- **Make a playbook.** As you develop the dashboard, write down the directions as you go so that they are fresh and so that others can follow your example. You know the dashboard best—help them learn it, too.

Notes:

_____

_____

_____

_____

_____

_____

_____

_____

_____

_____

_____

KNOWLEDGE SHARING—LEARNER TEACHES THE CLASS

Goal: Flip the learning by having the employees teach the class, learning the information at a deeper level.

Type: Qualitative

Ease of use: Easy

Explanation: For areas that involve training, this activity is a simple, effective (and cheap!) way to train.

- **Learning Pyramid.** Ever wonder why you're being lectured to and wonder how much of it you'll retain? Chances are, it's a small amount. In fact, the retention rate has been measured, and you're right, it's not much—about 10 percent! (See Learning Pyramid 2017, and Figure 5.2.) By contrast, people who teach information retain about 90 percent!

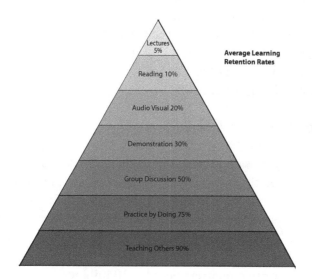

FIGURE 5.2. Learning Pyramid (Source: National Training Laboratoris, Bethel, Maine)

Using this knowledge, have employees (students) teach different parts of the class—make them responsible for not only their own learning but the learning of others. How do they know that the knowledge has been learned?

Notes:

_____

_____

_____

_____

_____

_____

TALENT ENGAGEMENT ZONE—PETITIONING TO ZONE? TIME TO REZONE?

Goal: Use the Talent Engagement Zone (TEZ) information to give employees focus on increasing their zone level.

Type: Qualitative (training session)

Ease of use: Moderate difficulty

Explanation: This is a training session that you can tailor to the group, strengths, and results of the TEZ. The assumption is that there is room for employees to grow (i.e., not everyone is in the green TEZ).

Potential suggestions and key points:

1. Where are they?
   - Do they know their strengths?
   - Do they use their strengths?
2. How much do they know about themselves?
   - Does the leadership team know their teams' strengths?
   - Are team members allowed to use their strengths?
3. Where do you go now?
   - Embrace change in your zone.
   - You can have it all—just not now.

Activity: How to get to the next zone.

- Have a brainstorming session in which individuals think up ways to use more of their strengths or to develop them specifically at their current job (5–10 minutes).
- In groups of three or four, have group members share their ideas and the pros and cons of trying to implement those ideas—such as manager resistance, lack of time, or lack of resources (15–30 minutes).
- Have individuals develop their own action plans with timeline actions such as two weeks, two months, or two quarters out (15–20 minutes).
- (Optional) Individuals can share project plans with the class as a method of confirming their commitment (15–20 minutes).

Notes:

_____

_____

_____

_____

_____

_____

_____

_____

_____

_____

TEAM IDENTITY—BUILDING A TREE

Goal: Achieve relative understanding of your own team as well as other teams around you.

Type: Qualitative

Ease of use: Easy

Explanation: This activity can evolve from the DIY group of assessments. The idea is to reveal how the team members see themselves. Give each person in the group paper and a pen. Have each of them:

1. Draw a circle the size of a soda can in the middle of the paper. Label the inside of the circle with the team's name.
2. From the circle, draw three lines leading in different directions from the center circle to three new circles with the words "physical," "cognitive," and "social" in each. These become part of your trees (see Figure 5.3).
3. Have team members enter ideas on the trees such as "works in Atlanta," "works on the second floor," "works by the café," and "works on the road" for physical; "does accounting" and "project managers of IT" for cognitive; and "works with market-ing—a lot" and "baseball team of great players" for social.
4. Compare the trees and the identity of each person related to the team and look for similarities. Some people will have similar characteristics (e.g., "works in Atlanta"), but others will differ vastly from one another. The goal is to build on the trees that most align with the company—its culture, values, or even guidance for working with customers. For those characteristics that are different, encourage the team to brain-storm and work to update and modify those to center the department's team struc-ture and cohesiveness.

FIGURE 5.3.   Example of Team Tree Building

Notes:

_____

_____

_____

_____

_____

_____

_____

_____

_____

_____

BUILDING STRENGTHS AND TALENTS, STEP 1—GETTING TO KNOW THE STRENGTHS

Goal: Learn strengths and skills of others and relate them to your own.

Type: Qualitative

Ease of use: Easy

Explanation: This activity and the next two are meant to be starting points for development of strengths and talents. A lot of information can be found on the Internet, and it is recommended that you find the activity that bests suits your group.

1. This activity works best after you have performed an assessment so that each individual knows or has a list of his or her own strengths, motivations, or other skill sets.
2. Discuss the activity with the team, either as part of a regular meeting or in an individual training session.
3. Give each person a list of his or her strengths from the assessment.
4. Tailor discussion questions around overall goals of the project and organization.

Notes:

_____

_____

_____

_____

_____

_____

_____

_____

_____

_____

BUILDING STRENGTHS AND TALENTS, STEP 2—FINDING THE DIFFERENCES AND MAKING THEM BIGGER

Goal: Understand how different employees on your team work—and how to work together in spite of (or because of!) them.

Type: Qualitative

Ease of use: Moderate difficulty

Explanation: Now that each employee knows his or her strengths, conduct a follow-up discussion on how to most effectively leverage the strengths and how to tailor the strengths of each individual to the team and to the goals of the organization.

- Make sure to review what can happen if an individual uses too much of a certain strength—if taken out of context, it can frustrate other team members. For example, I have a strength of asking questions—trying to get to the bottom of things. However, if I don't pay attention to how my questions affect my team members, I could ask too many questions and reduce my influence and my team's support.
- The level of difficulty is listed as moderate for this exercise because if it is done right, it can be uncomfortable for some to think outside the box or, outside their normal job description. What if you were in HR and an accounting analyst asked to help with your job? On the surface it doesn't make sense, and you as the HR manager may feel uncomfortable in granting the chance to the accounting analyst.
- Don't be afraid to ask the difficult questions and to allow feedback to be applied in both directions. You never know what you don't know—until you ask.

Notes:

_____

_____

_____

_____

_____

_____

_____

_____

_____

_____

_____

BUILDING STRENGTHS AND TALENTS, STEP 3—CONSTANT WATERING
Goal: Set up a process to continue to work on strengths and skills.
Type: Qualitative
Ease of use: Moderate difficulty
Explanation: This activity is simple in description—find a process that continues the work you've done in the previous steps. Keep up the momentum and continue to help employees do what they do best—their strengths, skills, or areas they enjoy that would benefit the team or organization in addition to their normal job.

- Your challenge will be fitting this process in with all of your other daily tasks.
- The best way to accomplish this step is to ask your team members how you can best help them use their talents to their full potential.

Notes:

_____

_____

_____

_____

_____

_____

_____

_____

_____

SETTING ACHIEVABLE AND MEASURABLE GOALS

Goal: Use employee-manager collaboration to identify top three goals.

Type: Qualitative

Ease of use: Easy (hint: repurpose the strengths from assessments)

Explanation: Sometimes the employee does not know the best way to use their own strengths, could be inexperienced, or simply does not understand the organization well enough to know how best to contribute. The manager can help by sharing high-level goals for the organization or team. Break those goals into consumable chunks so that the manager can identify specific opportunities for the employee to create alignment between the employee's goals and the organization's vision.

- Using a checklist of SMART goals (specific, measurable, actionable, relevant, and timely) could be a beneficial approach if a framework is needed.

Notes:

_____

_____

_____

_____

_____

_____

_____

_____

_____

ADDITIONAL ACTIVITY 1—OTHER ASSESSMENT ACTIVITIES?

We've given you a list of activities to try, as well as a list of assessments (see Chapter 3) such as the Success Scale, Utrecht Work Engagement Scale (UWES), Career Anchors, Myers-Briggs Type Indicator (MBTI), Standout, and What Motivates Me. As you go through your own TEO project, jot down effective activities you've tried here—and don't stop there! Help others by sending them to me at ashley@squarepegsolutions.org, and we will share your successful activities with others!

Goal:

_____

_____

_____

Type:

_____

_____

_____

Ease of use:

_____

_____

_____

Explanation:

_____

_____

_____

_____

_____

_____

_____

Notes:

_____

_____

_____

_____

_____

_____

_____

_____

_____

_____

ADDITIONAL ACTIVITY 2—TEMPLATE BASED ON YOUR TEAM CONTRIBUTION/NEEDS
Goal: What is the desired result of this activity or task?

_____

_____

_____

_____

_____

_____

_____

Type: Will the outcome be quantitative (numbers) or qualitative (words)?

_____

_____

Ease of use: How difficult is the task or activity to complete? Easy? Moderately diffi-cult? Highly difficult? Factors that may affect ease of use include the number of people involved, the number of steps, and the amount of work needed.

_____

_____

Explanation: As much as possible, explain specifically what needs to be done to attain the goal listed above.

_____

_____

_____

_____

_____
_____
_____
_____
_____
_____

Notes:

_____
_____
_____
_____
_____
_____
_____
_____
_____
_____
_____

ADDITIONAL ACTIVITY 3—TEMPLATE BASED ON YOUR TEAM CONTRIBUTION/NEEDS

Goal: What is the desired result of this activity or task?

_____
_____
_____
_____
_____

Type: Will the outcome be quantitative (numbers) or qualitative (words)?

_____
_____
_____
_____

Ease of use: How difficult is the task or activity to complete? Easy? Moderately difficult? Highly difficult? Factors that may affect ease of use include the number of people involved, the number of steps, and the amount of work needed.

_____

_____

_____

Explanation: As much as possible, explain specifically what needs to be done to attain the goal listed above.

_____

_____

_____

_____

_____

_____

_____

_____

_____

Notes:

_____

_____

_____

_____

_____

_____

_____

_____

_____

_____

5.4 Real Stories

Building a Plan Through "Actionable Components"

International business partnerships present a unique set of challenges, especially for small businesses. I was working with a client who was excited about a potential partnership with a business in Dubai, but apprehensive about pulling the trigger on the deal. He clearly spoke about the potential gains in exposure and revenue and showed me the SWOT (strengths, weaknesses, opportunities, and threats) analysis he had completed as part of his due diligence.

First, we dissected his SWOT results. We reclassified a few of his ideas into the correct SWOT quadrants and identified a few more factors, mostly in the threat quadrant. After our review was complete, he was still excited and a little more apprehensive. We proceeded by asking a very simple question: "What would make you more confident taking this to you partners for approval?" After a long pause and several shoulder shrugs, he talked about the importance of having tangible evidence of potential success.

With this feedback, we reverse engineered our plan by starting with what a finalized partnership would look like and then we broke down the actionable components of the partnership. Beyond the financial commitment, these included marketing efforts, new business development, introductions to other markets in the region, and coordinated meetings and presentations.

After our sessions, my client had a Skype call with his potential partner, informed him what he was doing to prepare to initiate their partnership and asked his counterpart to begin taking specific actions. Nearly six months after that Skype call my client had received several promises, and zero tangible actions to fortify his confidence and inspire his partners to agree to the partnership. Based on the plan that he committed himself to, he terminated the relationship and transitioned his focus to other potential partnerships.

—Michael Reddington, CFI, Vice President of Executive Education,
Wicklander-Zulawski and Associates

Building for the Future: an Action Plan for Managers

As a manager or a supervisor, we have the responsibility to our co-workers to support them and provide them opportunities for growth. There are several skills of an effective manager that reflect on them in a positive manner and that others around them will work to attain. First and foremost is for the manager to have an understanding and knowledge of job assignments, duties, and skill sets of those they supervise. This will allow them to provide guidance and technical resources to be more effective in their work on a daily basis.

The next responsibility is for the manager to provide the employee with an opportunity to learn about the responsibilities and duties of the manager. This will allow the employee some insight and the manager the opportunity to observe the employee in that role and possible future assignments. Additionally, this would allow for coverage in the event of the manager's absence, if necessary. Lastly, the manager should not feel threatened by an employee that has developed or attained their skill sets as a manager.

In fact, the manager should encourage the growth, promote those skills to others on the team and above and use the opportunity to learn from the employee. The worst inaction of a manager is to not recognize or support the employee for their efforts or skills. The worst action is when managers ask their employees to complete tasks the managers could have completed themselves, if they had further developed their own skill sets. In that scenario, the manager should feel threatened, unless they can recognize this issue and work to correct it. Otherwise those in their group will not see them as an effective manager.

—Rich Sevilla, as Acting Supervisor with the City of Newark

Combing Scattered Pieces: Building a Plan for a Large Group

An international manufacturing company who was preparing to begin a big international project needed assistance in bringing management employees from five countries to Charlotte, NC, to learn how to work together as one large team.

Although I've done team building numerous times, the challenge was that the company wanted all 60 of its representatives trained together at the same time. Typically, I keep the number to 20–25 for such a program for a successful team plan. When we sat down with the leadership and discussed all topics to cover during this training, it was clear it would take a full two days of training. Still, we were committed to help this company pull this large team together.

Since these 60 individuals hadn't met or worked together before, my associate and I built an action plan to give them an assessment ahead of time so we could quickly become familiar with the individuals' differences and similarities. I added this information to the company's requested strategic topics to develop a workbook/manual, specific for the course, but also with information that would make a good reference for later.

Using the information provided from the assessments, we selected physical and mental exercises scattered throughout the two days and placed strategically in areas to emphasize a point or support some of the lessons for these employees. These exercises also helped keep attendees alert and engaged. We also arranged the room to encourage good exchanges and to help the group get to know each other.

I asked the project manager to begin this two-day workshop to welcome and address the group with any comments he felt were important. Then I stepped up and asked the group if they understood why they were here. Surprisingly, most said no. I responded by relaying the importance of getting to know each other better and learning the material since they would now be working together as a large team.

By noon of the first day, we were already receiving positive feedback on the information being shared and activities used. The first focus was discussing results of the assessment and explaining how each employee had differences and similarities and to be aware of their preferences indicated and the like. This portion of the program was very helpful for most. All feedback supported the value of our program, which greatly benefitted the company as they began their large project. I saw this as a successful action plan. It was critical to understand what the company wanted to accomplish, and to order the topics appropriately and allot sufficient time.

—Robyn Crigger, CEO, Compass Career Management Solutions

CHAPTER 6

Putting the Action Plan into Place and the Keys into the Ignition

6.1 The SBSG Story

"Hey, Heather, how are you today?" Joe asks as he follows her into the conference room on Thursday for the weekly director/leader team meeting.

Heather, the director of accounting, barely nods, her eyes focused on her seat at the table or, more appropriately, the seats around her unofficial "assigned" seat. She is looking for those on her team who are missing from their unofficially assigned seat (assigned by her, of course). It is two minutes before start time, and everyone knows that Heather's team has to be there five minutes early—before her—or they would hear about it. Luckily for her team, at least on that day, they make it in time.

"Oh my," thinks Joe, taking his own seat (neither assigned nor the same as last week or the week before that).

He looks across the table at Julia, the VP of HR, and receives a small smile and a wink with a look in Heather's direction. He had talked through Elizabeth's TEO project and proposed action plan with Julia yesterday, and it went well. His primary goal was to get her buy-in for HR, but he had the unexpected benefit of a mini prep/mentor session.

Julia had explained what an organizational-development intervention looks like (because it appears he might need one!) and the three types of intervention. He was basically trying to get individual buy-in and support by working on influencing using an "individual intervention."

His goal at this point is to have the key department leaders understand the purpose of the TEO project—its value for them *and* the requirements (money, time, people) needed. He is well on his way with two of the five directors, and he had an additional touch-base meeting with the executive team (that, fortunately, Julia was on). Once he has achieved his goal, he feels he can give Elizabeth the green light for going forward with the TEO action plan.

He looks across the table and tries for a smile from Heather again. "Hmm," he thinks. "She's a big Astros fan ... let's start there. Find common ground."

6.2 The Nuts and Bolts

High five! The hard part is over, right? You did the initial review, you've analyzed your data, you found trends, and now you have an action plan in place. Well done. It's time to *get the plan started!*

Before we set off to the races, Lightning McQueen, first make sure you're starting the race set up for the best possible finish. Let's take a look one last time at what you've done and how it aligns with what we said we're going to do. Now that we have the action plan in place, we'll make sure that the executives are on board.

The final part—and arguably one of the most important parts—is making sure the teams or individuals are ready or at least prepared for what will be happening (from the action plan and potentially outside of it, such as steps that can take longer than planned) in the next few months.

Step 1. Set Priorities

If you had to summarize the top two or three goals your action plan will accomplish, what would you call out? (Examples: gain four hours or 10 percent more per person on my team, improve communication on my team so we do not lose a customer's order in one week, or improve team knowledge in planning and organization). List them below.

1.

_____

_____

_____

_____

_____

2.

_____

_____

_____

_____

_____

3.

_____

_____

_____

_____

_____

Next, explore how those accomplishments are tied to your goals. (See Chapter 1.3, "Activities and Application," or Chapter 5.2, "Nuts and Bolts," to review your recorded goals.) How do your top two or three items relate to your goals?

_____

_____

_____

_____

_____

_____

_____

_____

Finally, prioritize. If you have a more robust action plan, you will have several tasks and assignments. Go back to your action plan and prioritize which tasks are most important. Let's say you plan to complete the project in three months, but then your company decides to purchase another company and needs your help in moving through the acquisition process in one and a half months. Therefore, you will have only half the time to implement the action plan—how are you going to use that time? Rank the tasks in your action plan from most important to least important to help you organize the steps. You may not tackle all of them, but you can first address the low-hanging fruit and then return to your plan after your successful merger (that is, of course, if you haven't been promoted for the amazing job you did; then you'd have a great action plan for your replacement!).

Step 2. Get Executive Buy-in—Again

It can be painful to talk to the powers that be, especially when you're trying to convince them to use the company's time or money. Articulating your plan to them can feel political or like navigating a minefield of words.

A bit about corporate politics: It can be said that management is all about playing the right cards at the right time. Others may describe management as simply working the system or the game. Both depictions have a negative connotation. Politics happen at all levels of life, and it's not an inherently bad thing. Rather, it is a way for us to bounce ideas off each other to come to an optimal conclusion and fair compromise.

Intel offers its employees a grounded ideology known as "constructive confrontation." In a nutshell, it basically encourages employees to think through their proposals thoroughly and to defend their positions. This simple practice encouraged growth and opportunity, which may be one of the underlying causes for Intel's 2,400 percent stock increase between 1987 and 1997 (Conner 2013).

It is my humble view that most healthy versions of politics are blends of marketing and emotional intelligence. Knowing who your audience is, what motivates them, and where they are in their current situation are key factors in a successful relationship. By knowing your audience and their motives, you can play the right cards to appease all sides of the organization and leadership. In doing so, you've also created a pathway for yourself to make a difference and flatten the hierarchy. If you show your audience the research you've done, you should have a fairly compelling case to convince them of your plan's more efficient use of the company's time and money.

First things first. At the beginning, you secured initial confirmation from your executive team (see Chapter 1). As a quick reminder to yourself, the team members signed up for the following:

_____

_____

_____

_____

_____

_____

_____

Since you were thinking ahead, you also set up check-in points—times when you would check in with the executive team (via e-mail or phone or in person). If you haven't already set those dates, do so now.

_____

_____

_____

_____

_____

_____

_____

Now that you are at the agreed-on point, you should write a short, two- or three-bulleted summary on the results of the assessment, trends, and action plan thus far. Note the "bulleted" part. Executives do not have a lot of time, so focus on the key areas.

To start, let's think about the big-ticket items. What are the three key areas you want to focus on?

Hint: Go back to Step 1 where you listed your top priorities.

1.

_____

_____

_____

_____

_____

2.

_____

_____

_____

_____

_____

3.

_____

_____

_____

_____

_____

Now, list the information that is pertinent to the executives. Are they focused on the cost impact? The time it will take? Who will be involved? Relate each of the three areas to the points most relevant to the executives.

Priority/Action Plan Item Area of Impact/Relevance

1.

_____

_____

_____

_____

_____

2.

_____

_____

_____

_____

_____

3.

_____

_____

_____

_____

_____

Finally, talk about how you will measure your success, how you will succeed, how you will review progress from here, and how you will adjust the plan as needed:

1. Criteria for success (how you will succeed)

_____

_____

_____

_____

_____

2. Metrics (comparison of before and after)

_____

_____

_____

_____

_____

3. Progress updates (how you will communicate updates, what you will communicate)

_____

_____

_____

_____

_____

4. Plan adjustment (how you will adjust the plan if needed)

_____

_____

_____

_____

_____

You now have the elements to communicate to your executive team. You have built a solid platform of the critical goals and priorities, described how they relate to the executive's goals and focus items, and shared the structure of the action plan through metrics, updates, and adjustments. From here, you can summarize this information in an e-mail or expand it into a presentation based on your previously agreed-on plan.

Step 3. A Prism of Buy-in—Looking at the Action Plan from the Perspective of Other Individuals and Teams

It's time for round two—getting buy-in. You may decide to skip this section. After all, you already have buy-in from the senior team. But wait. Did the team members buy in to the entire project, or only the idea of it? Did you do what you said you would, and is it the same thing they pictured you would do with the money and resources (yourself, your team, and any other assets)? It's crucial to ensure that all stakeholders have bought into your vision and that you have their undying support. Set up accountability for yourself by sharing your vision and goals with them so they can also be a part of the journey with you.

This section focuses briefly on the senior team, which we have already discussed, and also on five other groups that you should consider:

ACTION PLAN IMPACT: THE BUY-IN LIST

1. Executive team (round two)
2. Peers
3. Those who don't know you or who are in another department
4. Those who are senior to you
5. Those who work for you
6. Those you don't know very well

Note that these groups are not mutually exclusive, meaning that people affected by the change could fall in several of those groups. Use this section as a reference to address potential issues, ideally *before* they happen. Feel free to also reference this section if you are being challenged by someone in this list.

Finally, note that one group is missing from the list: individuals who do not accept the action plan or change. Not having the support of all stakeholders is common; you will have the ability to work with them and get through the challenges in Chapter 8, "Roadblocks." The following recommendations are for the individuals who are, generally speaking, more likely to adopt your plan when you present it in favorable terms (i.e., a little more "logically").

1. Executive Team (Round Two)

This section is a summary because both Chapter 1, and the previous Step 2 in this chapter address how to gain support from the executive team. Since you have done most of the work by this point, you are now armed with data, specific information, and an action plan—so the goal of securing buy-in from this team is to do the following:

- Review the information that you provided before (as needed; some teams don't need this).
- Update team members on the highlights of what you have done since first presenting the plan to them.
- Briefly cover the plan and next steps.

- Explain how the planned successful outcome will be reached, and when they should expect to see the next response and results.

Round two may take place in a meeting, a phone call, or an e-mail. However, if you have the time and ability to get this second buy-in, you will get further and be more successful in the end with this team's approval and buy-in. Remember that your input is valued even if you are not part of the C-suite. An organization will not ultimately succeed unless it supports its middle managers and identifies their progression and ability to change. They have a unique insight that the leaders of the company do not have—that of knowledge from their direct connection with customers, vendors, and peers (Ashford and Detert 2015).

We are working on getting your action plan accepted and getting you ready to actually *take action*. If you're like me, you were ready to go three chapters ago but are humoring yourself reading these chapters. (It's a good thing too, I promise.)

Here are three ways that you can improve your chances of obtaining buy-in from all groups:

- **Find meaning.** Everyone is motivated by something. Sometimes it's obvious, overt: I want to climb the ladder, take a new job in Seattle, work as few hours as possible, and still get my paycheck. Some are a little less obvious. The CEO should focus on the bottom line, whereas the sales department's number one motivation should be on sales, but that isn't always the case. Understand your stakeholders by learning their perspective, what drives them, and ultimately, *what's in it for them?*
- **Remove doubts.** Change initiatives are hard for most people (take a look at Chapter 2 for a few examples of why), especially if they come from people you don't know or understand or who have different perspectives. Find out about their concerns—and address them. Find ways to stop their doubt, or address what their ultimate concern is. Almost always, the change is never as bad as employees think it will be, but addressing employees' fears head-on will help them accept the change as well as the steps and tasks needed along the way. Focus on the problem statement and then offer your proposed solution and your estimated derived benefit.
- **Know your audience.** Are the individuals who will be impacted by the action plan and the changes couch potatoes, 5K people, or Ironman runners? Do they accept, move, and train slowly, or do they take an idea and head for the hills before you even get to the "how to"? Make sure to align your action plan to their speed—or a slightly faster speed. If it is a large change (for example, altering a software or benefits package), consider a full communication strategy in your action plan and make sure there is enough time for individuals to absorb those changes.

2. Peers

Your peers typically are most like you and are going through the same things that you are dealing with; they understand what you are going through—typically.

Your peers could be your easiest group to convince, so if you know a few who could be early adopters, then approach them with your plan. Approval of your ideas will likely gain momentum and boost your confidence, which will help you in your efforts with individuals who may not be as quick to adopt.

In some cases, you may have to watch for jealous peers who see the innovative work you've done, or the visibility you are having with the project, and want it for themselves. Again, you probably know this audience and can prepare accordingly—use your best judgment here. You just need a small group for your initial experiment to polish the rough edges and fine tune before sharing it with higher-ups.

3. People Who Don't Know You or Who Are in Another Department

People who haven't worked closely with you may need assurance that you have their best interests, and those of the organization, at heart. Past change initiatives and their promoters may have made them wary. I've been there. I've worked in a few departments in which consultants (internal or external) or directors from another department said "Hey, I've got this great idea," and proceeded to try to implement it in my department. No talking, no discussion. They had no idea what my department was about and didn't ask us what had been done. They simply issued commands. In each case, the plan ended up being terrible because the consultants had missed key parts of our processes— they didn't know or care to ask.

Sounds like fun, right? (Insert sarcasm here!) It happens all the time. So, for those who are on the receiving end of your action plan, remember—they haven't walked a mile in your shoes. They don't even know what your shoes look like. They haven't looked at the data, and they certainly don't know the results (yet). Bring them along. Talk with them about what you've done so far and what your plan is. Better yet, work with them on the action plan in case they see parts that need tweaking. You may still end up with a few people who don't support the plan, and if so, it may be time to visit Chapter 8. For now, grab the early adopters and the ones who aren't (overtly) against it and keep moving.

4. People Who Are Senior to You

This group encompasses people who are senior to you but not part of the executive team. Of course, theoretically, people who are senior to you (especially in your hierarchy or chain of command) should be the first to support you since they typically serve as the go-between for you and the executive team. However, I have worked with people whom this group did not support. Sometimes people in these intermediary roles do not know what is going on around them and fail to observe that *their* bosses actually support initiatives promoted by people at lower levels.

At the end of the day, you want your leaders to look good. Bring them along as much as you can. Copy them on e-mails, stop by their office, and update them with good news. Your plan may not be first in their mind, but work on at least getting it in their mind—somewhere. Perhaps consider a mentor relationship with someone senior to guide you through the process of having your initiative accepted and to also offer a bridge of communication to the executive leadership.

5. People Who Work for You

On the one hand, these people work for you, so they should support your plan at least in respect of your position. You sign their evaluation, so it pays to support the boss.

On the other hand, they may have reason to question you as a leader. If you are, say, always implementing something, your team could wear down from change (your changes) and numbly follow you. They are not advocates for your work and may slow you down.

Treat this group as you would with any other—follow the three general guidelines as listed in the first part of this section ("Executive Team, Round Two"). Find meaning for your employees, remove their doubts, and know your audience.

6. People Whom You Don't Know Very Well

You do not know these individuals in the organization or have ties to them, but you have to work with them to change the organization through the action plan. In general, you have information about them (perhaps through the assessment or another reference point). If these individuals are relevant, or could have a different perspective on your TEO project, spend some time with this group if you can, either as individuals or as a team. Have an information lunch or coffee with them so you can get to know them. The more they can trust you or your team, the more likely they will be open to listening to and accepting your suggestions and changes when the time comes.

6.3 Activities and Application

Step 1. Priorities

You've got the action plan. What are the key points? How are they tied to the goals? (See Table 6.1.)

Steps 2 and 3. Getting (and Confirming) Buy-in

This step is all about getting people on board with what is changing and with what you're trying. You don't have to have all the answers, but employees have to understand where you're going and what you're trying to accomplish along the way.

How will you secure buy-in from others? What challenges will you see? (See Table 6.2.)

6.4 Real Stories

Engaging Strengths and Overcoming a Difficult Project Buy-in

At my previous consulting firm, we were leading a large transformational project to achieve cost reductions for a major US retailer. I was leading the operations category and was working with a cross-functional team. Our initial workshops and store visits had gone well; we had a solid list of cost-reduction hypotheses that we would soon turn into recommendations after additional analysis and validation. Unfortunately, the procurement director assigned to my project often missed key meetings ... I assumed this was because he was busy with his day job. We got to the point where we needed his agreement to confirm our preliminary list of cost reduction opportunities.

TABLE 6.1.   Application Step 1

KEY POINTS	GOALS	SUCCESS WILL LOOK LIKE ...
Example—Building empowerment in the team members for their own talents	Increasing talent engagement in individuals in the finance department	Increased talent engagement zone score by 20%

At the next meeting he dropped a bombshell: "Unless this group supports my idea to outfit all items in our warehouse with this technology then I will tell the steering committee that I support none of this." He had previously raised the idea of investing in this technology, but the business case didn't justify us making this recommendation as a part of our cost-reduction project. The investment was quite high, and it would take a long time to recoup the benefits. I was taken aback at first … I was surprised at how open he was with this ultimatum. I tried at first to explain that we used a standard cost-benefit analysis for each of the opportunities and that his idea didn't make the cut. He wouldn't budge on his position, and the meeting ended uncomfortably.

I then scheduled one-on-one time with him the following week. Before speaking about the project, I first asked him how his day job was going and what were the latest firefights that he was engaged in. He expressed his high level of stress on the job: that

TABLE 6.2. Steps 2–3

GROUP	CHALLENGES FOR BUY-IN	HOW YOU WILL OVERCOME CHALLENGES AND GET SUPPORT/BUY-IN FROM INDIVIDUALS AND TEAMS
Executive team		
Peers		
People who don't know you well/are in another department		
People who are senior to you		
People who work for you		
People you don't know well		

the initiative my consulting firm was leading was one of several that he had been asked to participate in. He griped about his boss and how he frequently made unreasonable demands. I correctly guessed that it was his boss that was pushing the initiative for the costly technology on all items in the warehouse. I then had a flash of brilliance. I said, "Given your knowledge of the procurement costs and their volatility, I think you would be in the best position to present our final recommendations to the CFO." He immediately saw that this would be a great way for him to get exposure to the executives. He had aspirations of moving up in the organization to a larger role in our department but he felt stuck under his current boss.

I immediately saw a change in his behavior. He became much more invested in our project and contributed to all of our group meetings moving forward. He took ownership of the cost-benefit methodology we used and agreed that the high investment cost of the project wasn't right for this initiative but could be right for a future initiative. I coached him before the final presentation, and he did an impeccable job when presenting to the CFO and the steering committee. The recommendation was not a part of our presentation, but I believe he made it happen the following year. By highlighting how this project could be an avenue for him to shine in front of corporate executives, I quickly turned an enemy into an ally.

—Dan Gagne, Senior Manager, EY's Transactional Advisory Services

Getting Buy-in: Old School versus New School

In the early stages of a lengthy leadership development engagement for a distribution company I encountered an old-school manager who was openly resistant to our efforts. He made several antagonizing comments in front of the group, made himself an obstacle in a group exercise, and was clearly trying to rally others in the group to join his cause.

Thankfully one of his outbursts involved a good idea that integrated well with part of a previous exercise. I was able to publicly reinforce his idea and his thought process, which created the first crack in his armor. This crack gave us an entry to help him internalize the necessary changes while protecting his self-image. I immediately placed him in a leadership role within the training sessions that allowed him to see himself as an authority figure within the group and forced him to verbalize the thought process of the teammates he represented. We continued to have robust conversations, and over time it was clear his perspective was changing.

The final day of our engagement involved obtaining feedback from senior executives regarding the participants' progress and all of the participants submitting a lengthy case study. The feedback from this gentleman's senior executive was so positive that it surprised both of us. Perhaps most surprisingly, this gentleman's final case study was the second highest ranked submission out of the entire group.

—Michael Reddington, CFI, Vice President of Executive Education,
Wicklander-Zulawski and Associates

Lead by Example: Jumping in to Buy-in

When leading a team, it is always important to lead by example. Working with teams of 10–300 associates, the best way that I have found to gain respect is by being willing and *able* to do all of their daily tasks. Working in a warehouse environment, it has been immeasurably valuable to always come prepared to get into the process. That means having the safety equipment on hand and having the presence of mind to identify need before being asked. The difference between taking 30 seconds to solve a problem and taking five minutes to find someone else to do it is massive! Not only does it give you instant credibility, but it levels the organization and humanizes you as a manager.

With an organization that often utilizes 50 percent of its manpower in indirect roles—or roles that support the associates adding value to the product—there are countless opportunities to jump in and make a difference. The impact I have seen with one hour in the process is far greater than what is seen when simply filling the role with an hourly associate. If you have built respect with your team, they will rally around you, making you a force multiplier and driving results.

—Paul C. Terbrueggen

An Action Plan built to Recover from Running Aground

BACKGROUND

I was finishing my first command tour when one of the ships in the squadron ran aground. The commanding officer had been removed for cause, and I was detailed to fill a gap in leadership pending the arrival of a replacement. I was keenly aware that there was a need to evaluate and profoundly change the focus, if not the entire command climate. In addition, my commodore wanted "more heads to roll." This left me in the position of having to build trust and unit cohesion while simultaneously satisfying my commodore's desire to eliminate people he felt had contributed to the event. The ship was in an overseas port, and the crew had been shell-shocked by not only the grounding, but also the loss of a very personable and likeable commanding officer (who was more interested in being their friend than their leader). I was left in a position where I was seen as a grim reaper intent on racking up a body count and doing the bidding of higher authority. In short, I felt that I was not trusted and, honestly, I was not keen on blindly trusting the crew.

WHAT I PERCEIVED

Recognizing that the trust deficit was deep, I immediately set out to repair the relationship with the crew. On the other hand, I had to get buy-in from my commodore for rebuilding the team. I felt that he was more focused on accountability and retribution than repairing the trust among the new commanding officer and his crew.

WHAT I DID

I gathered the crew and told them that nobody was going to get fired as long as they were honest with me. I gave them 24 hours to reveal any and all facts about the grounding that they had been told not to share. I then explained to them that there were rigid standards of performance and that we were going to hold ourselves to those standards. I explained that we were merely custodians of the ship and that the rules were literally written in blood spilled by those who had failed to follow standards. I called my commodore and told him my concerns about trust and what I had done to repair the trust deficit. I began paying attention to the smallest things. Morning quarters (morning meetings within teams) were reinstated, uniforms were standardized, haircuts were required, planned maintenance was accomplished and the workarounds to make life easier (at the expense of safety) were cancelled. At first the crew bristled with this new focus on requirements, but we gradually began building expectations of performance. An acceptable standard was established. My commodore was less than thrilled with the idea that I had essentially begun an amnesty program for the rest of the crew, but I found that he was grateful for the information the crew provided about the grounding that enabled the squadron to learn what *not* to do.

WHAT HAPPENED

A month after taking command, the ship returned to home port. The crew was very nervous about what had happened. In spite of being the senior officer in the group, I was assigned a pier space that was both inconvenient and had a reputation for being a penalty box for poor performers. I refused to tie up and demanded that we be given a place on the pier. The crew watched as I dug in and explained to my commodore that this was a crew of qualified and dedicated sailors who had been through a lot, who were willing to work to get back on track, and who did not deserve to be treated as pariahs. We got our pier space, and I told the crew to walk proudly, set standards, and pay attention to the little things like the way the lines holding the ship were laid out, the cleanliness of the pier, and I demanded that they wear ball caps with the ship's name. I kept them in three-section duty (on duty overnight every three days), but I allowed them to build plans to address personal issues and instituted a plan for professional development for every member of the crew. I took an active interest in them as professional mariners and curtailed my predecessor's plan of being everyone's buddy. Six months after taking command, it was time to turn over the ship to a new commanding officer. My commodore had retired and his replacement never saw anything other than a top-notch group of professionals. My crew saw their advancement rates double (25 percent got a promotion), and the day I turned over the ship, the crew gave me a special boat paddle with fancy knot work and embedded symbols of the ship.

THE FINAL REWARD

The best gift I ever received came almost a year later when the crew was given the battle efficiency award for the squadron, which means they had come from being perceived as the worst ship in the group to being considered the best team of warfighters in a squadron full of top-level performers. The rules allowed me to share in this award and to this day it remains one of my most personally satisfying achievements in a career spanning 32 years of service.

—*D.P. "Skip" Shaw, Captain, US Navy, Retired*

SECTION 4

Getting There... Is It Possible? (Transforming the "How")

CHAPTER 7

Checkup—How Are You Doing?

7.1 The SBSG Story

It has been about two months since the start of the TEO project. For Matthew, who works for Elizabeth and is a manager of six—it has been long enough. He's been working for SBSG for about four years and has moved up to manager from where he started. He fought the changes at first, and Elizabeth listened to his objections. She explained the reasons for the plan, the projected outcomes, and what the company potentially had to gain as the employees went through this process. She then worked side by side with him as she started rolling out some of the changes.

The changes were small at first—reducing the number of times during the day that employees should check e-mail and increasing the number of one-on-one meetings with the direct manager. Matthew did think the mandatory one-on-ones were annoying at first, but did buy in once Elizabeth eventually explained why.

The changes have grown in size and impact as the action plan continued (Elizabeth always talks about the TEO-AP—the talent engagement optimization action plan, as she called it). The changes have become more focused and, to Matthew, a bit more uncomfortable. For example, Elizabeth wants to know what he wants in a job and how he could get more out of his role.

He has never been asked those questions before—in 10 years at multiple companies. It has never occurred to him to think about them.

What's next? How would he know where these changes and his job would end up?

7.2 The Nuts and Bolts

If you've followed the talent engagement strategy—your TEO project—to the letter, you're entering the third phase and the third month of your project. Things are either going really well, or you are starting to see some problems (we'll talk more in Chapter 8).

Your action plan is in action (from Chapter 6), and you're probably already seeing some of the fruits of your labor—in this case, improvement in the system, in people's attitudes, and in work capacity. The changes in your action plan could be incremental; it could be in leaps and bounds.

A key element to the success of this project is consistency—in making sure that the tasks that need to be covered are, in fact, covered and that action is carried out accordingly. You created a timeline to complete the tasks and a list of who should be doing what when. As cliché as it sounds, slow and steady wins the race. You're better off using smaller, measurable, yet consistent approaches than making drastic overhauls. In the process, you are also able to identify which parts of your solution are making the most impact so that you'll be able to scale your plan accordingly.

But Are Things Going Great? Really?

Take a look at the action plan now and at the items that still may be a few weeks or even a month or so away. Now look at items that are owned by people who are not close to the project or not as invested in the results of the project. What is the chance these items will be completed on time? What items are in the red of a red/yellow/green status—and do you know it? (Note: Red/yellow/green is a status used in project management to show where you are in a project.)

Just as managers must invest time in their people, you must invest time in the project. *Continually check, survey, and assess the situation.* This advice holds true not only for your TEO project but for any project that takes multiple steps, an action plan, and other people to implement.

Have You Asked the Right Questions?

Have you asked the right questions in your information gathering or assessment to gather the data you need to make an informed decision?

Are you able to convert the inputs you received into actionable items? This is where the qualitative and quantitative data become your way of assessing the organization's health—checking the pulse—with respect to talent engagement. What kind of energy is your organization observing based on this assessment?

I'll tell you a story. I was once worked on a project—and I was sure it would succeed. We did the testing, we checked the numbers—it worked! When we tested the new process with different employees, it went well and the employees seemed to like it—so it was going to work! (And, by the way, the project was going to save our company about $10,000 in the first three months!)

However, I never followed up. Once my team finished the project, a few brave souls kept the project going for a few days. They tried—they really did—but after about a week, all of the work my team had spent so much time on had disappeared completely. I went back about three weeks later, ready to bask in the glory of the great work we had done, and found that *nothing* had changed since before we implemented the project!

Moral of the story: your plan takes constant watering. You don't have to micromanage every step, but you do need to keep an eye on the development stages to look for problems that may emerge (see Chapter 8 if they do).

Why the Best Plans Fall Apart

Do an Internet search for why projects fail and you'll find myriad reasons. For the most part, the articles are written by people who have "been there, done that, got the T-shirt."

The lists below comprise two key groups of reasons that projects fall apart. The first three deal with how you set yourself (and the project) up for success, and the second three deal with getting the right people on the right page at the right time.

1. Missing the Process
   a. Lack of clear goals or vision (International Project Leadership Academy 2017).
   b. Lack of visibility (West 2017).
   c. Scope creep (Stewart 2015).

2. Losing the Team
   a. Poor communication (Carlos 2015).
   b. Working with the wrong people (Trigg 2015).
   c. Lack of accountability (Marr 2016).

Let's briefly talk about each one.

1. MISSING THE PROCESS

You spent a lot of time at the beginning setting the vision for the project and making sure you had visibility, telling others in the organization about the project. You knew exactly what the scope and purpose of the project were. Geneca (2011) found that up to 75 percent of software and business projects are expected to fail for these very reasons. People inside the organization didn't know or understand the purpose of the project. They didn't fully come along for the ride.

But don't panic: You don't have to start over—you've been working through these steps as you went along. This is a good time to check up on what you've done so far and look for any holes. Review your goals. How do your current goals compare with the ones you initially set? Are they the same? Have they changed?

What about visibility? Do you still have enough eyes on the project by people that are not directly involved with the project—but buy in or support it?

Are you still doing what you said you were going to do? Did other problems come up? (They probably did!) How did you handle them? Did you put them in a parking lot for a future task?

Remember, the goal of this section is to gain perspective on where you are. Don't let the project get away from you—address the issues. See Part 7.3 for guidance in thinking through the issues.

2. LOSING THE TEAM

More than likely, when checking the state of your project, if you do find bumps in the road, they will probably be related to the last three items in the list above—dealing with people. Change is hard. Dealing with people becomes inevitable in the process of creating positive and effective change within the organization.

Communication is the easiest challenge to address—and the most difficult to consistently get right. You can communicate through e-mail only to have your team want an in-person discussion. You can then discuss in person, only to have the items requested for a memo sent via the intranet. You should continually get a pulse of the team and the organization that you are addressing. It might also be worthwhile to consider what kinds of communication are better received in person versus through e-mail, and vice versa. How can you also make sure that the information being relayed is not only well received but acted on?

WHAT IF YOU DON'T HAVE THE RIGHT PEOPLE?

That is a challenging question, but it's part of the point of the talent engagement. You may have the right people but maybe you have not yet tapped their motivation, resources, or capacity. The easiest way to address this issue is to focus on what they are doing well and build off that. If an individual's strength (from their CliftonStrengths assessment) is focus and you need to deliver an action plan task next Wednesday, then focus the person on that task, and then on another one, and so on. Consider this—your goal is to figure out what makes each person tick. What is the secret code, combination, or answer that motivates and gets each to be the most effective person each person can be?

Accountability may seem the most difficult of the three, but it can be the easiest—as the beginning and end lie with you. What will you do if someone does not complete a task? How will you check up, follow, continue, tag, and respond? Will you e-mail his or her boss? Send a polite note? Tell everyone on the team if someone fails? You must follow the guidelines of your company (that is, don't tell everyone if a polite private e-mail is the normal procedure).

HOW TO HANDLE CHALLENGES AND SETBACKS

Half of the battle is being aware of what's happening. You now know the main areas to watch for—continue to check up on these. We will be measuring the results in Section 5, but you should continuously be tracking and looking to make immediate changes as necessary as feedback rolls in. This agility will help you as you continue the project.

If you find yourself running into problems such as pushback, a reduction of capacity or productivity, or challenges in the form of more questions (or fewer questions in the form of reduced engagement), read Chapter 8 in which we'll talk about roadblocks, interventions, and how to manage both.

7.3 Activities and Application
1. Missing the Process—Questions to Ask Yourself

Goals: How do your current project goals compare with the original ones? Are they the same? Have they changed? How do you or should you address them so that they are connected to the success of the project?

_____

_____

_____

_____

_____

_____

_____

Visibility: Do you still have enough eyes on the project by people that are not directly involved with the project—but have buy in or support of it?

_____

_____

_____

_____

_____

_____

_____

Scope creep: Are you still doing what you said you are going to do? Did other problems come up?

_____

_____

_____

_____

_____

_____

_____

Parking lot: What other areas, problems, or issues came up during the action plan implementation? Put those items here and reference them for a future project.

_____

_____

_____

_____

_____

_____

_____

2. Losing the Team—Questions to Ask Yourself

Communication: How do you communicate your action plan to the people involved? What is working? What is not? What needs to be changed?

_____

_____

_____

_____

_____

_____

_____

Working with people: How do you know if your people are buying in to what you're saying? If they are not, or if they seem to be the wrong people for the project, how will you help each one maximize his or her capacity and engage in the action plan at the same time?

_____

_____

_____

_____

_____

_____

_____

Accountability: How do you hold people accountable for their actions? What do you do if an individual did not complete a task by the deadline? How do you reward (if necessary) individuals who complete action plan tasks on time or early? What is your company culture or accepted norms for doing so?

_____

_____

_____

_____

_____

_____

_____

7.4 Real Stories

Following Up—Giving Time, Setting Expectations, and Ccelebrating Success

The concept of "following up" can be a lot of things, but a key success factor is to flesh out the project scope prior to a launch. Clearly defining what success looks like in terms of outcome, timing, ownership, checkpoints, communications, budget, priority, and general expectations sets the stage for clear accountability, objective discussions, and laser-like focus. Sounds easy, right? Well, factor in the experience of the team leader and members, staff development objectives, group dynamics, business environment, management support, and the like, and it becomes apparent just how important this prework is for success.

As a project sponsor, define what the expectations are for progress updates—what needs to be communicated, how frequently, and to whom. Have an upfront discussion on how to handle surprises and issues—they will occur. This sets the stage for fact-based discussions and opens the door for seeking help. It also helps create a positive environment for coaching and development. Plan to dedicate time, particularly in the early stages, to get and keep a pulse on the project's progress and coach accordingly.

Give credit publicly and reference the project's impact on customer needs or business objectives. Document the learnings and outcome—celebrate successes. So, a word about a recent application of these concepts. To give an example, a project was conducted on processes associated with receiving goods into a small distribution center. The approach taken was to make this a very quick-turn _kaizen_* burst, targeting a reduction in processing time. Additionally, we took the opportunity to make this a development exercise for the kaizen team members. Setting the stage for following up was key to making this project a great learning experience for the entire team.

How did it work out? At the beginning, you do not clearly know what can be achieved in any kaizen project, but, in this case, the team achieved a whopping reduction of over 160 percent of the targeted reduction in processing time. Home run! Additionally, the success of this project led to a company-wide workshop in which everyone received training on kaizen concepts and then created a target list of opportunities to reduce waste—across all functional areas of the company. The broader implications of this event link directly to some of our business objectives around teamwork and faster response times while lowering costs.

—*Greg Winn, Director of Technology and Continuous Improvement,*
White Knight Engineered Products Inc.

* Kaizen is the Japanese word for "improvement." In the business world, it takes on the meaning of "process improvement." For purposes of talent engagement and TEO, it's a tool you can use to implement your action plan. See Chapter 10 for more information and how to apply basic techniques.

Knowing the "Why" Can Be Just as Important as Knowing the "How" When Checking on Your Team

A third-class petty officer is a first-line supervisor who will typically supervise three to five very junior sailors. Before I could be promoted, I had to take a leadership course that was being taught, in part, by a master chief petty officer (MCPO). An MCPO is the most senior enlisted rank in the Navy, and this particular master chief was very senior, as master chiefs go. He told the class that soon, we would be petty officers and be charged with the awesome responsibility of leading sailors. He said the most important thing we could do was to take care of our people; give them the tools to do their job, listen to their concerns, and solve their problems so they could do the work while we supervised the work being done.

He went on to tell us a story of when he was a young man and on a cleaning detail. The supervisor of the cleaning detail was a second-class petty officer who was a bit overbearing and drove the sailors assigned to him pretty hard. One morning the petty officer gave out the work assignments and told our young master chief to clean the shop truck, inside and out, with the fire hose on the side of the building. The master chief said he had been very frustrated working for the petty officer but tried to clarify the instructions that he was given.

When the master chief began to ask the petty officer if he was sure he wanted the truck cleaned, inside and out, with the fire hose, the petty officer cut him off and told him to do what he was told. At that point, the master chief was tired of being talked down to and had tried clarifying the instructions, but the second-class petty officer was adamant that the master chief just needed to do what he was told. So the master chief did.

The master chief opened both doors of the truck and began rinsing out the inside of the truck cab with the fire hose. The second-class petty officer came running out of the building when he noticed what was happening. He began yelling at the master chief and said "You're going on report." The second-class petty officer's supervisor was called, and when he arrived, he asked the master chief why he had used a fire hose to clean the inside of the truck. The master chief explained what direction the second-class petty officer had given and explained that he had tried to get clarification and was yelled at and told, again, to do what he was told. So, he did. The second-class petty officer ended up getting written up for his poor leadership.

The master chief finished his story by saying "You need to understand that people are fundamentally good and want to do a good job. If they have a complaint or a question, there is a reason for it and you, as their leader, need to listen. Either the instructions are confusing or flawed in some way, or there may be a reason the instructions cannot be followed; in any case, there is a problem that the sailor's leadership needs to resolve."

I will never forget that lesson. Taking care of the people who do the work that needs to be done in an organization is paramount. And listening is the best way to understand what we need to do as leaders to care for our people.

—Sam Pennington, Captain, US Navy

CHAPTER 8

Roadblocks

8.1 The SBSG Story

It has happened. The TEO project is working well in the HR and operations departments—they were on track, and positive results were coming out weekly, if not daily, from the managers as well as the employees. Elizabeth, as the TEO project leader and also as the operations manager, can almost see the project's finish line with those groups.

The accounting and marketing departments, however, are other forces to be seen. Joe has warned Elizabeth that Heather, as director of accounting, would be pushing back, but they don't expect it to be at every single detail—especially when Elizabeth's team is trying to help the accounting team improve (to have more time in their day and enjoy their work more). Joe believes that Heather is worried about losing control of her team, and therefore (overtly or covertly) some people on her team aren't doing the requested items on the action plan. Elizabeth isn't so sure.

The marketing department is a different, and somewhat surprising, story. Led by Mary, the marketing director, the department became extremely defensive when the project was proposed. Elizabeth and Joe wondered if team members were concerned that the TEO project would reveal areas they weren't doing well in—that Mary, as director, wasn't doing well in. The individuals are set in their ways and were comfortable with the way things were. So, the TEO action plan is not going forward as expected.

When Elizabeth started what she thought would be a simple, positive organization project, she never thought it would become a battleground between departments and teams. Was that what was happening? How can she now address it?

8.2 The Nuts and Bolts

It has happened—you're two or three months into the plan, and you hit the dead-end feeling. You can't go any farther; the road you are on just turned to that sticky mud that makes moving in any direction worse—not better.

Perhaps your assessment went well—you were able to involve several different teams—and you conducted the assessments without any problems, gathered the results, and even interviewed several members from each group to give you a well-rounded approach to your data. You found some trends; for example, you learned that people who were not engaged failed to see the results of their work being measured. They also wanted to work outside of the scope of their job description by even adding tasks that would support the organization's initiatives. You went back to the executive team members and got buy-in support to continue the project—albeit, they did seem a bit distracted when they said to move on to "phase two."

Now, phase two is a disaster. Although you still have at least a month or two (or longer) on your TEO project, you just received an e-mail saying you have been assigned to a new project that may take 85 percent of your time, in addition to the three other projects on your plate.

You've received pushback from two of the five teams that you're working on—from the leaders themselves—who believe the action plan work is superfluous and not helping anyone. The two leaders want to have a meeting with the other three leaders to convince them that the project is not helping the organization, and you just happened to hear about the meeting from "someone in the know."

Where Do You Go from Here?

You, my friend, are not alone. You are the reason I wrote this chapter—and I've written it from the school of hard knocks. I would venture to say that no good project or action plan gets accomplished without at least one roadblock, if not more. You've hit a roadblock, but you can turn that roadblock into a mere speed bump. Keep reading.

Perhaps there has been poor communication. Perhaps the number of agenda items on your plate makes the day dictate what you will do as opposed to you dictating your own schedule. Regardless of the roadblock, it's holding you back from implementing a valuable strategy that has been proven with qualitative and quantitative analysis. To create your own path, you may need to do a few hacks that may include blocking out focus time on your calendar, creating your own plan of action, or preparing for distractions along the way.

Why People Push Back

I was once assigned to a large, highly visible project that the executive team of the company directed. It was a rollout of a new operations plan for a certain area—and it had to be accepted by over 30 buildings (and specifically, the building leaders) within four months.

You would think it would be easy to tell these 30-plus leaders to implement the project because the CEO said so, but as many of you know, that's not the way it goes (think of how far you got if you said "because Daddy said so" over and over to your brother or sister). You must be independently able to deliver on the transition message on your own—otherwise, those leaders will work only so hard as they are "seen"—meaning they will revert back to what works for them as soon as they can.

I was on my own. I had the data behind me, and for the most part, about 80 percent of the leaders were OK with the changes requested; they were not hard to implement, and they would not impact the leaders' organization that much. However, the final group of five or six leaders did not want to implement the changes. Even after explaining what the CEO wanted from them and then telling them they had to carry out the changes because they would be held accountable for their own results, I was met with grunts, grumbles, and defiance. These leaders were two or three levels senior to me—and some didn't feel the need to give me a reason as to why they said no. They just did what they wanted.

This was the first time I had been in a situation like this, so at first, I took it personally. They *will* do what I say because I am the messenger for the CEO! But where would I end up with such an attitude? Only far enough for them to show me, as the project leader, enough so I would leave them alone. No more. I had hit a roadblock. (Actually, I hit a number of them.)

So it was time for an intervention (more on interventions later). I needed to examine their individual concerns and the goals they had for their teams to figure out how to help them.

I spent time with each of them, not really asking them questions but following them around and listening to them do their work, their way, in their organizations so that I could begin to understand their problems and learn how this change would impact their processes. I could see just how messy these changes were going to be for their teams to make. I wouldn't want to make them, and I was instructing them do it, just because the CEO ordered the changes! These changes would slow down their organizations, and what they were rewarded for was going to be penalized because of this new process.

Armed with this new information, I put a new action plan together. The change would happen after the allotted time frame (it was an automatic switch), but we changed the way it would impact these particular leaders and their teams by adjusting the way they did their work. The solution wasn't a perfect match—there was still some pain in the transition, and the process wasn't 100 percent better overall—but their needs were heard and addressed.

This story reflects two of the main reasons why you hit roadblocks: fear of the unknown, and people who don't understand your situation trying to make changes that affect your team. The next section addresses several of the most common roadblocks you may encounter and a few suggestions on how you can address them. Chapter 8.4 shares other stories that may help shed some light on roadblocks and help you realize you're not alone in facing them!

If you have your own roadblock stories (and how you overcame them), please share them by e-mailing me at ashley@squarepegsolutions.org for the next edition.

Often, the most challenging part about creating change is guardrails—or limiting the scope of your project. If the changes you propose are spread across multiple departments in the organization, then you'll need to attain buy-in from each of those teams. This may create a long, winding road to reach the destination point of your action plan. You may want to keep the implementation small at first and then scale based on positive results.

You Have the Power—To Create an Intervention

WHAT IS AN INTERVENTION?

If you don't have much knowledge of business interventions, you might be visualizing personal ones: a man's friends getting together to tell him that he needs to leave his clingy girlfriend, or a woman being told by a gathering of family members that she should become an artist and leave her banking job.

In this case, we will apply the term to the organizational-development viewpoint—in that the intervention is an event or series of events to change the status quo to help or improve the current operation (for example, the process, people, culture) to better the company for a certain purpose (Anderson 2015).

There are typically three types of interventions:

- **Individual.** Coaching, leadership development, anger management, goal setting.
- **Team.** Team building, small-scale group culture changes (such as a process improvement program in the operations group).
- **Organization-wide.** Strategic initiatives, large-scale culture changes (such as realigning the company during a merger and acquisition), product line rework (bringing new products in or eliminating others).

In a general sense, the project that you have delivered this far is an intervention of a type. You have decided to *intervene* with individuals or a group to redefine how they work, are assessed, and interact with each other—with the result of changing their behavior at work.

An intervention does not have to have a negative connotation.

You're now at a standstill. Something has changed. Something may have faltered with your initial project, and it's time to assess and create an intervention. In Part 8.3 you'll find some suggestions and a checklist of ways to do this.

THE BASICS: HOW TO PIVOT

A quick (final) word about roadblocks. You are not alone. You are not a failure if you reach this chapter, after a great assessment, buy-in, or implementation plan, only to find no one wants to do the work. Many people get here—it's a bit of human nature. Now, it's time for the rubber to meet the road.

One way to get past this wall you're facing is to realize that you expected this. Change affects people in different ways, and knowing ahead of time that you will experience interference or pushback will help you be prepared when it happens—and set a course that doesn't include bandages and tears.

Now you're ready. It's time to *pivot* or take a different viewpoint. Answer these five questions:

1. What is the source of the problem?
2. Who is the source of the problem?
3. Does the goal need to change due to changes since initially setting the goal?

4. Has something happened since the action plan was set that redefines what's impor-
    tant in the action plan and its result?
5. Who do I have that will support me with this pivot?

_____

_____

_____

_____

_____

_____

Each of these questions takes the "one step at at time" approach to the overall problem.
Work on these questions in the Activities and Application section and begin developing
your pivot plan. After answering the questions above, you'll have to prioritize where to
begin. The analogy of small and big rocks comes to mind. Tackle the bigger issues first
and then knock out the smaller roadblocks—one at a time. In doing so, you're creating
an easier path to success with your value proposition.

Typical Roadblocks

Sometimes all you need are a few examples. Take me, for example. If you teach me one
way to swim (let's say, the freestyle stroke), then I'll figure out a few other ways to prevent myself from drowning (it may not look as nice as the backstroke or butterfly, but
I'll stay afloat!).

The following is a collection of the typical roadblocks with groups of people and a
few suggestions on how to approach them (see Table 8.1).

Lack of buy-in

In Chapter 6, we focused on six types of people who voiced their support for your
plan. For continuity's sake, we will stay with these six types, but will group them a bit
differently:

	GROUP A	GROUP B	GROUP C
Group (from Ch 6)	1- Executive Team 4- Those senior to you	2- Peers 5- People who work for you	3- Those who don't know you 6- Those you don't know well
Roadblock type	Overlapping (multiple) roadblocks—depending on external factors outside of the project	Tend to see you from the same vantage point. They may have history or experiences that could benefit or hurt your roadblocks	Greatest unknowns—you know the least about them so you may or may not have to work harder to convince them

TABLE 8.1.   Roadblock Groups

GROUP A	Executive team	People who are senior to you
GROUP B	Peers	People who work for you
GROUP C	People who don't know you or are in another department	People whom you don't know very well

The following seven areas focus on different ways your action plan and results can be blocked. Keep an open mind and perhaps a hazard sign handy as you wade through some of these common project roadblocks.

1. LACK OF INITIATIVE

Initiative is about taking responsibility for your part of the project, work, or task and making it your job, your focus, to make it excellent. It is about going the extra mile and instead of asking "What is the least amount I can do to call it quits?" asking "How can I best help myself, my fellow employees, team, boss, or company be the best through what I'm doing?"

How it should be done. When you work with different people (and this applies to all the roadblock groups mentioned previously), you want to clear the way for an open forum. Design each discussion session about the action plan to involve as much collective brainstorming as possible. Keep your own knowledge and areas of expertise in mind when thinking about what the group is working on. How can you help? How can you uniquely contribute?

OK, well, that's great—but you're not the problem. Right. You have taken initiative from the beginning. It's the other people who don't want to help or think, let alone think outside of the box. You want to work with someone with initiative: a self-starter, someone who's proactive, someone who's persistent and won't rest until the project has met his or her high standards. Finally, you want someone who is curious and has imagination.

Here are few ways to help motivate people to take more initiative:

- **Brainstorm ways—ask.** Just ask the individuals how they would do the project, the change, or the task differently.
- **Suggest they put themselves in their customers' shoes**. In this case, they should focus on the results of the project or who will benefit from it. What do their customers want? Need? In what ways?
- **Define who the customer is**. Sometimes this task is the hardest. Some people may see the work in the action plan as just that—work—and not realize that they are helping others. Help them see the way. Who needs the services they provide? Why? In addition, help them see that "customer" may not refer only to an outsider—but to a peer, a boss, or even another department.
- **Suggest they look for problems to solve**, such as procedures or policies that are out of place, and areas they could help improve in the action plan. Just because you built the action plan doesn't mean that's the best way to manage it.

Note that the line above says "help motivate people to take more initiative." The wording was carefully crafted there. You cannot *make* anyone take more initiative. People have to want to do it themselves.

2. CHANGING PRIORITIES

Oh, this one is a fun one, isn't it? Your boss, let's call him John, gives you this great project to lead. You build the assessment plan and the action plan, and you're moving down the road. All of the sudden, John changes your priorities. The action plan isn't gone, it's just supplementary, not as important.

Or, you still are the lead, but the two or three people who have been instrumental in carrying out key tasks (working within their department, for example) have had their time appropriated.

You can recover. The best part of the action plan—and how you've developed it—is that it is a living, breathing, working document. Go back and look at your timeline. Assess the people and areas that will be impacted and adjust.

In the end, if you have to expand the project from 100 days to 125—or even 200 or 365 days—you are coming closer to TEO, and every step helps. It may just take longer to get there.

The idea is to keep the core of your action plan alive. Something else to think about as you're building the action plan—is it time sensitive? Creating flexibility is a part of preparing yourself for the inevitable roadblocks ahead. Cover your bases as much as feasible.

3. LOSS OF FUNDING

The concept of loss of funding may result from changing priorities. Maybe you have no resources—in the form of time or tasks—to get things done. There could also be a drop in support from roadblock Group A (people senior to you) because *their* priorities have changed.

Don't sweat it. There's a lot going on in the levels above you, and you're only going to be privy to some of it. Take it in stride, and see what you can get and where you can go from there. What *can* you get accomplished? Think about a few negotiation strategies here. Can you agree to cutting back a quarter of your time, and finishing 5 of the 15 tasks you said you could do in that time? You could think about the action plan in terms of chunks of time—how can you successfully complete part of it and maybe negotiate for something later?

In any project, you have three primary resources:

- Features—the elements in your proposal that you're suggesting to add or amend in the organization.
- Time—it takes time to make any implementation go live.
- Money—there is a dollar amount attached to what you want to implement, whether it be costs or benefits from the proposed value proposition.

These are the three resources that you will have to use in your negotiations. It's up to you to weigh the costs and benefits associated with leveraging these resources to see your project to completion. The negotiation strategy should try to focus on efficiency—yielding the most results with the least amount of expense (time or money). After you establish the positive yield, then you build leverage to request relatively smaller features to your proposal after earning the trust of the management team.

At the end of the day, *how* you choose to negotiate will depend on your audience. Cater your presentation to the target leaders based on what you know about them. Are they the kind of leaders who support large-scale changes? Or do they want to spend the least amount of money for as much change as they can receive? Assess them before stepping into the ring. Ask your peers who may have worked with them for advice so that you can better understand their personal style.

4. Pushback

Handling pushback is both easy and difficult at the same time. Pushback has been discussed several times (in Chapter 1 and Chapter 7), mainly with regard to roadblock Group A that works above you in the hierarchy. What if others push back?

Roadblock Group B—people who are your peers and juniors—more than likely are pushing back because they don't know enough about the situation or are concerned about change. Change is difficult for many, and the more that individuals feel that this change is being pushed on them, the more they will push back. Review the concepts in Chapter 2 and consider the way you are sharing the information. Are there ways for them to contribute and for them to take initiative that will give them a voice? (See "Lack of Initiative" above).

Roadblock Group C, consisting of people who are in unfamiliar territory, need one thing to begin—familiarity. The more information you can give them—the more willingly they will contribute to their part of the action plan.

Change is challenging. As creatures of habit, we have natural apprehensions about going against the tide. Oftentimes, we don't even question why things are the way they are. We just assume some invisible logic led to a plan or policy being instituted.

That is where you come in. The world is ever-changing, as is every industry and every team. The dynamics will differ over time. Your proposal should account for the inevitable changes that will occur as a result of your plan.

5. Less capacity or productivity than before the action plan

Ouch. This is one roadblock that makes me cringe when I think about it—it's happened to me often, and it always creates a few kernels of doubt about my project and planning before I move forward. I have done all this work—and all of the measurements, the surveys, or feedback at the halfway point are showing that the measurements are *worse* than before, or at least, certainly not better!

You've done the assessment. You've got the buy-in and the action plan, and the project is moving. You're nearly done … but there are *no results in sight*. Nothing that shows that you're getting more of the metrics you deemed to improve when, where, or how you said they would. You want to grab a paper bag and breathe deeply … or find your resume and start looking for a new job.

Before you start hunting for a new position, here are a few possibilities for why:

- *There hasn't been enough time to see the results.* This is highly probable if you have a smaller number of participants or you're moving the needle, so to speak, in a smaller way. Think of the people on shows like *The Biggest Loser*—they are able to lose

10 pounds or more every week in the beginning. Yet later, even losing one or two pounds is a struggle. The closer you are to the goal, the harder it may be to see it. Give it a bit more time.

- *The current results look worse than the original ones.* This can easily happen, but don't dispair. You may have *measured the current results a different way than the beginning results.* Are you looking at it apples to apples—in the same light? For example, did you add the same number of people, in each category? If you're using an Excel sheet, is the formula calculating the right numbers? If not, try stepping through the calculation by using the function "Evaluate Formula." I can say this as I've done it more times than I have fingers. Your best bet is to go back and check the numbers. Make sure that the formulas work and that you're calculating the numbers the same. Are they units or cases? Individuals or team?

- *Something else has changed during the time that has affected the results.* This one may be the most difficult as it could have a subtle impact that you may or may not see. What if 15 percent of the people in the group left during this time due to a reorganization? Is it enough to change the data? Possibly. You could potentially go back and adjust the data or you may need to find a creative way to estimate how to compare the two groups.

The bottom line is don't panic. If this is your first scaled project, know that this is a common occurrence and that you may just need to change the perspective slightly. There is a chance that some projects don't work, but the reason is typically due to other issues. You may have to spend time on this to understand the impact and if a reassessment is needed.

The key is to remember that you have qualitative and quantitative analysis to back your value proposition. If you know you did your research well, you should be confident in the yields of the project. It's also important to remember that "negative" yields can still be a good thing. At the very least, you'll learn what happened unexpectedly that you hadn't initially accounted for and be able to amend those in the following version of your project.

6. MORE QUESTIONS

The final two roadblocks—more and fewer questions—are on opposite ends of the spectrum. You may ask why both are considered roadblocks. Shouldn't one be a good thing and one be a bad thing?

Well, yes. However, both in large amounts can slow or stop a project.

In this case, more questions initially sounds like a good thing. People from the various roadblock groups are coming at you, asking "How does this work?" or "What can we do about this?" or "Have you thought about that?"

This is great! They are taking initiative and giving ideas, right? Or are they? Are they slowing you down, pushing back, and giving vague or bogus information by asking all of these questions and redirecting your path?

Potentially. If they are in Group A—they are senior to you—they may be generally curious. Respectfully answer their questions and settle their concerns so you both can move on.

If they are in Group B—they know you—they could be individuals that want to slow your project's progress. Focus on the low-hanging, easy fruit. For those who keep asking "why" after you've answered, let them know you'll respond to their questions but that you have to move on now.

If they are in Group C—the unknowns—give them some time. These could be your breadwinners, the ones who will support your cause and make the action plan a success. If they really are asking too many questions, find a way to address their concerns, maybe in a forum or at your office. You want them to know they have an outlet (instead of complaining to other people about you or your project!).

7. FEWER QUESTIONS

So, you're looking at a room full of no one. It was supposed to be a quick Q&A session on the results of the assessment—the next steps for the action plan—but no one came.

You continue on the action plan but get nothing. You send e-mails, and no one responds. You talk in person and barely get feedback.

The lack of response could be because the action plan is not high on anyone else's priority list (see the "Changing Priorities" or "Loss of Funding" sections above) or they just don't have the time. It could be a peak season or a time they have blocked off for other projects. Find out. Whether you know them or not, get to know them—take them to lunch and make it a little more personal. Learn more about what they are doing and find out how you can help *and* get the action plan accomplished.

It may help to start with a few key individuals. Approach them personally and ask for their support. They can be the ones to help you take the project to the next levels of the organization.

8.3 Activities and Application

Application 8.3a—Pivot Questions

When you are ready to pivot or take a different viewpoint, answer these five questions. You may find that you want to complete this section and proceed directly to 8.3b, which walks you through how to pivot using an intervention you select.

1. What is the source of the problem?

_____

_____

_____

_____

_____

2. Who is the source of the problem?

_____

_____

_____

_____

_____

_____

3. Has something happened since the action plan was set that redefines what's important in the action plan and its result?

_____

_____

_____

_____

_____

_____

_____

_____

4. Do you need to revise the action plan goal due to changes that have since occurred? Does the goal need to change due to changes since initially setting the goal?

_____

_____

_____

_____

_____

5. Who will support me with this pivot?

_____

_____

_____

_____

_____

Application 8.3b—How to Manage an Intervention

Anderson (2015) recommends five areas to consider when picking the right intervention strategy. When thinking about handling your roadblocks with an intervention, consider the following. Using your answers from the above section, select the intervention strategy that works (see Application 8.3c on intervention types).

1. Match the intervention to the data and diagnosis. Is the solution big enough for the problem? Or is it too big?

_____

_____

_____

_____

_____

_____

_____

_____

2. Consider the employee's readiness for change. Can you use communication (for example, discussion in meetings) to help?

_____

_____

_____

_____

_____

_____

_____

_____

3. Understand and then make a decision on where the intervention should start. Where is the biggest problem? Should you meet with the senior team or individual contributors? Should we try to fix the easy problems or the big ones?

_____

_____

_____

_____

_____

_____

_____

_____

_____

4. How big of a roadblock is it? What is the depth of the intervention? Using Reddy's
    (1994) levels, consider where is the right place to start:
    The work itself.

_____

_____

_____

_____

_____

_____

_____

Easily seen team issues—conflict, communication issues.

_____

_____

_____

_____

_____

_____

Not easily seen team issues—culture, power struggles.

_____

_____

_____

_____

_____

_____

Values and beliefs.

_____

_____

_____

_____

_____

_____

Biases that people are unaware they have.

_____

_____

_____

_____

_____

_____

_____

5. In which order should the intervention go? You can start anywhere (see number 3 above), but what is the main goal of the intervention? Is it:
    Acquiring more information?

_____

_____

_____

_____

_____

_____

Becoming more effective in the action plan?

_____

_____

_____

_____

_____

_____

Becoming more efficient? Faster?

_____

_____

_____

_____

_____

_____

Staying relevant to what's going on in the organization?

_____

_____

_____

_____

_____

_____

Application 8.3c—Intervention Types

Table 8.2 provides an overview of the different types of interventions you may use.

TABLE 8.2.   Intervention Types

INTERVENTIONS	INDIVIDUAL	TEAM	ORGANIZATION/COMPANY
Types	Assessment, coaching, one-on-one development, feedback, training, playbook development	Team training, group feedback, team development processes, team meetings, process restructuring	Organizational changes, strategic adjustments, corporate hierarchy changes
Why intervention needed	Growth potential of leader, prevention of firing of employee, succession planning, individual conflict issues	Department reorganization, problems within a team, misalignment of tasks, lack of communication	Benefits rollout, M&A of pre-existing companies, introduction of major system (MRP, Six Sigma) or new department
Who can help	Manager of individual, potentially peers and direct reports	All people in team/department, potentially other departments that have a great impact on that team	Primarily senior leaders, should have some input from employees at all levels in organization
Potential results	Reduction of attrition, creation of career succession plan, increase in employee capacity of individual or leader	Reduction of team conflict, increase in group productivity, reduction of communication problems	Less resistance to major organizational changes, faster adoption and return on investment (ROI) impact of change

8.4 Real Stories

The Constant Nature of Roadblocks

Roadblocks are a constant in business. If not for roadblocks, we wouldn't have problems to solve and challenges to overcome.

I have found that roadblocks take two key forms:

- Actual business and operational roadblocks.
- Cultural and mental roadblocks.

The first one (business/operational) is actually easier to overcome than the second one (cultural/mental). How many times you have heard "Great idea, but it will never work here" or "This is how it has always been done here" or my favorite "This is not the culture here!" If these roadblocks become critical to business success then any amount of consultant help, technology, and process improvement won't help the business. To overcome this roadblock, you have to use a two-pronged approach:

1. Build a coalition of like-minded folks and demonstrate with small controlled tests and implementations that change can happen and is good for the business (critical mass).
2. Continue to win the hearts and minds of the naysayers with a series of small successes (critical momentum).

Critical mass and critical momentum will reach a level where successes become a trend and winning becomes natural! And guess what, everybody wants to be part of the winning team.

When I was tapped to transform a customer service organization in a very short period of time, I encountered numerous roadblocks including severe financial constraint, obsolete technology, siloed organizational structure, over capacity labor pool, and massive bureaucracy and red tape. But the most challenging roadblock I faced was the culture and defeated mind-set of the leadership team. This victim mentality has made the team afraid of taking risks, afraid of failing, and honestly afraid of even trying.

To me, this was the most critical roadblock I had to overcome. And it took a lot of effort and some time. But we overcame it by aligning the team around a cohesive strategy, creating a culture of test/fail/iterate, celebrating every success however small it was, celebrating each failure as lessons learned, implementing fun contests to boost morale, and finally, thinking outside the box. Once my leadership team became comfortable coming up with new ideas, testing them out in a small way, failing fast and learning from failures, and celebrating each success, their mind-set started to change—and quickly. With this boost in confidence and can-do attitude, they were able to tackle most of the business roadblocks as a collective team.

—*Ritesh Chaturbedi*

The Worst Roadblock: Downsizing Does Not Mean Down and Out

My story on roadblocks took place in a Navy recruiting district (NRD). The Navy Recruiting Command (the organization responsible for recruiting for the US Navy) had decided to reorganize all 26 recruiting districts into "divisions" with each division led by a division officer. Previous to this, the districts had been divided into "zones" with a senior enlisted chief petty officer in charge. The new construct was being implemented to solve a couple of problems—to unite officer and enlisted recruiting efforts to gain some economies of scale for our limited resources and to provide oversight by commissioned officers with a more balanced approach to the recruiting mission.

BACKGROUND

Navy recruiting is primarily managed at the lower levels by "career" recruiters; the group of sailors who undertakes this mission as their profession are known as the "career recruiter force" (CRF). Sailors can apply to become a member of the CRF community after they have successfully served a tour of duty as a recruiter. The CRF community is relatively small, very close knit, and run by leadership within the community itself. This change in direction came from an admiral who saw a need to have some oversight of the CRF community. This leader had a reputation of "burning" through the first tour recruiters. The methods were effective, but not at all efficient. Anyone who has seen the movie *Glengarry Glen Ross* may have an idea of how brutal the sales environment can be. Recruiting is a sales business.

Executing the change from zones run by senior enlisted CRF to divisions run by commissioned officers who did not have the technical sales background the CRF community had was difficult on many levels. The largest issue was the culture of the CRF community. I was the commanding officer of one NRD and had to realign 10 zones into eight divisions. There were many factors that drove how we divided up the territory.

Creating divisional lines on a map was challenging because we needed to ensure that everyone had a fair opportunity to be successful given the market we were creating for them. While we reviewed how we would redraw lines on a map to make up the new divisions, we also addressed the number of offices each division would have and took the opportunity to close some poor-performing offices where the market didn't support the investment in resources.

Closing offices was hard. I had to prove to my leadership that I had done the business-case analysis and could still meet my mission with fewer offices in the field. My basic argument was to throw fewer nets into the water but to throw bigger nets in areas where I knew there were more fish. The office closings were just one of many other factors that needed to be addressed during the district reorganization beyond the CRF community losing direct control over the mission that was their profession. In addition, there was the perceived insult of having a leader put in charge who had less experience and knowledge about recruiting. Understanding what needed to be done to effect the change successfully was a function of knowing the business. My team not only knew the details of recruiting processes, they knew the context of the details and how the processes had to be changed given a new paradigm where two missions were combined under one organization.

The reorganization was a success. We became more productive as a district, recruiting more people overall. We were truly more effective and efficient as an organization. As I worked through the planning and execution of the reorganization, I learned a few things about changing organizational processes, procedures, and reporting structures.

1. **Conveying a vision—the desired end-state—and the resources available to get to the end state are the two most important aspects to change.** Those two things will determine the "what," "when," and most importantly, "how" for achieving the desired change. Resist the urge to tell the people involved in the change how to execute. Letting the organization develop the solution within the resource constraints, in my experience, allows for the most creative, eloquent, and effective solutions.

2. **Ownership of the solution is critical for people to truly believe in the solution, but especially important when there is a real or perceived shift in authority or power.** The group whose power is being diminished must be a part of the solution. I leveraged my CRF personnel to provide all the technical documentation for the various markets to best define the new divisional lines. I also asked to write the new policies to ensure the change in leadership at the zone and divisional level was executed and accepted with respect to the daily processes involved in getting a prospective sailor through the recruiting process.

3. **Leadership must support the team; leadership must provide the organization with the resources it needs to execute the plan—time, money, and support.** Support could possibly be engagement with higher leadership to defend the solution the team built. When the team members see leadership caring for them and providing the resources, they will coalesce and be able to achieve more because they will trust that leadership is a part of the team. There will not be "us" and "them" within the organization, there will simply be the team.

4. **Expectations are important.** Leadership must convey expectations early, clearly, and often. Leadership must also actively work to convey the vision and determine if their expectations are being met. If expectations are not being met, leadership must determine why the expectations are not being met: lack of understanding of the vision, lack of resources, or some other issue that must be addressed. Change is not something that is requested and subsequently delivered; it must be managed, encouraged, and supported to be effective and meaningful.

5. **Sometimes people need to leave an organization for positive change to occur.** Despite everything above, some people will not be able to get behind the direction that leadership has set. Ideally, these people should leave the organization. If leaving the organization is not possible, these people need to be insulated from the work that is being done to effect the desired change. If naysayers remain within the organization in positions to influence others, they will slow or stop the desired change.

—Sam Pennington, Captain, US Navy

An Elaborate Success Plan—Overruled

I joined a new organization with the charter of instilling a product-management culture, taking the larger team (including my boss) away from a shiny-object mentality. The president of the business unit as well as the VP of HR said that they were worried about this team's deliverables and wanted me to lead them to a data-based, delivery-focused approach.

Based on my past background in change management, I was energized, excited, and could not wait to unleash new processes, mechanisms, and systems to kick-start the change management and herald the desired changes. I spent time meeting and engaging with my peers, boss, and stakeholders, identified key gaps, and came up with a series of recommendations and proposals. I was contented to see a complete nodding of heads when I proposed my changes but was later surprised when I started getting pushback. I was shocked when even my boss went around the elaborate steps I had developed with his consent and backing. Over time, my efforts were nullified.

I stepped back and evaluated the situation. I realized that my peers and leader were either not fully aligned on the vision and on the need for change management or they had concerns with my approach. I shared my observations and concerns with my boss who refuted my observations. He had counter reasons on why he had to go around our agreement. While I did not agree with all of his reasons, I realized that I had to change my approach to working with the team.

As next steps, I recalibrated my efforts, reached out to key stakeholders (the finance leader and peers who were open to the changes), and engaged them on an individual basis to get their commitment. I identified that this was an important initiative for all and not just me and wanted their inputs to make this successful.

I started my change journey again and this time I got more traction from the folks I engaged. We established what "good" can look like and shared the initial results with my boss and the rest of his direct reports. Over time, people saw the benefit of moving to a systemic way of prioritization and focusing on key deliverables instead of looking only at the latest technology that may or may not solve the customer needs. I then engaged with the senior leaders and shared my journey (both the good and not so good) with them and solicited their help in driving home the message.

The measure of success in this initiative will be when we have the entire business unit marching to the same steps (e.g., common methods, metrics, and cadence). Right now, 50 percent of the initiative is done.

A key learning for me, as an outsider, is that I needed to understand the culture, know the key players and observe their working styles first before making changes. Instead, when I brought data-driven facts and recommendations, people were overwhelmed as my no-nonsense approach was new to them. They were used to the one-to-one engagement model and multiple discussions (often with limited facts) before an agreement would be reached. They were not used to limited meetings with large amounts of data to make their decisions. Also, I learned to be aware of the difference in cultures and styles and that I needed to think in terms of handling this as an adaptive challenge without compromising my values.

—*Karthik Sivakumar, Senior Director,*
Product Management and Strategy

CHAPTER 9

You've Got Backup: Support in the Organization You Didn't Know You Had

9.1 The SBSG Story

Elizabeth looks at her computer screen and blinks in rapid succession. The training report in front of her is not getting done—even though she has been working on it for an hour. The facts and mostly figures of the high-level report are 75–80 percent complete, but the commentary, analysis, and background story were, well, just not getting done.

Joe has done a lot to *try* to get Heather's accounting team members to work toward their TEO milestones, but whereas members of other teams are in the 50–70 percent completion range for their milestones (meaning that at this point, they are on track to complete them by the 100-day deadline), accounting is at … 10 percent (really?!). And that figure is being generous—basically little more than writing their name on the milestone sheet and showing up to the first meeting!

Elizabeth feels a knock on the desk. Startled, she looks up. Justin is looking down at her with a goofy grin—his signature one (even if he doesn't recognize it himself).

"How ya doing, kid? Looks like you're thinking about 37 things right now."

She takes a breath and turns away from the monitor. "I've been better," she says with a wry smile.

"What seems to be ailing you?" Justin is currently serving partly as receptionist and partly as purchasing assistant manager for the company and sits fairly close to her desk. At work, they don't have a lot in common, but since they work in close proximity, they have developed a friendship. She has found out he has an amazing background: he was an instructor, an investigator, and an entrepreneur. However, it still surprises her that he is doing so little for the company now when he'd happily do so much more. In fact, he is one of her biggest TEO proponents.

She sighs. "The accounting department. I don't know how to get them to feel they are part of the team … or, at least certain individuals. I feel I've told them what they needed and why we're all doing it … but it seems to fall on deaf ears."

Justin laughs his (also signature) hearty laugh and grabs a chair from the desk next to hers. "Oh, you mean Heather? Heather and her clan?" Elizabeth says nothing; her facial expression gives her away.

Justin says, "Heather has a few things that must be done a certain way … but if you pass those wickets, then you may be able to break through and help her and her team understand the changes that are happening and why they would best benefit them."

Elizabeth takes out her notepad and begins to write, furiously.

9.2 The Nuts and Bolts

You've hit the midpoint, you may even be past the point of no return—meaning things can't completely go back to the way they were. However, with a few roadblocks and issues coming at you, you may feel a bit deflated or that you're slowing down or losing motivation. Don't worry. It happens to the best of us—and it's certainly happened to me.

In this chapter, we'll talk about a few theories and frameworks that can help you not only finish your TEO project with strength but also carry on after because they apply to many of the things you already do. Most of these tools you have either heard of or have worked with (but may not have known it). You may find them under subject areas such as organizational behavior, industrial and organizational (I/O) psychology, human resources, organizational development, or just plain leadership. The important point is that you can recognize them as tools for your success.

Note that not all of these tools will be useful—or useful to you right now. Use this chapter as a reference to come back to, and you may find a different opportunity each time.

We will cover many areas in a relatively short chapter. The topics move from areas that affect each employee (such as emotions) to larger areas such as group decision-making. This information is designed to whet your appetite; if you find that the topic applies to your TEO project or to the work you're doing, I would recommend researching it more in your favorite search engine.

Basic Emotions

This may seem the easiest of them all—you've had emotions since you were literally a baby, right? So why can't other people figure out how we're feeling (and handle those feelings accordingly)? Consider this scenario: You're giving a compliment to the individual on the team who you felt went above and beyond—and he storms off midsentence. Baffled, you turn back to your desk, scratching your head. What went wrong?

In 2015, Pixar and Disney released *Inside Out*, a movie about a young girl who spends her first years in Minnesota and moves to San Francisco, which becomes a fairly challenging adjustment.

The focus of the movie, however, is not only about what is happening to Riley, the main character, but also what is going on with the emotions in her head. Led by Joy (representing happiness), the team consists of Anger, Fear, Sadness, and Disgust.

The movie is actually based in a lot of truth. Paul Ekman, a psychologist who studies emotions, said that for the most part, there are six universal emotions: the five listed above (happiness, anger, fear, sadness, and disgust) as well as one more, surprise (Burton 2016). We won't spend much time on them since you're probably well acquainted with them.

The research on emotions is wide-ranging, and everyone from psychologists to business leaders focus on the results of the impact of emotions at work, and how to best interpret and use them properly.

So, in the example above, you intended to display happiness, but your employee may have perceived that you were surprised by his good work, which therefore made him feel a completely different emotion—anger—on the other end of the spectrum. You can sometimes mistake disgust and anger, but rarely will you mistake either of them for surprise or happiness (Robbins and Judge 2014).

How does this scenario tie in with your TEO project? You may find yourself in situations with people you don't know, and you may not know how to read their emotions. As a result, you could find yourself at odds or in conflict with another person. A *conflict* is any situation in which your concerns or desires are different from another person's. So, in terms of emotions, conflict could be a difference of viewpoints, emotions, or experiences. Trying to understand where the other person is coming from will help your progress in the action plan.

Also, politics at work is natural to the industry—any industry. To me, handling politics at work is understanding other's viewpoints and managing *to* those viewpoints (and expectations). We've all heard the importance of knowing your audience before preparing your pitch.

However, what does that mean? Understanding your audience's emotional behavior is important to shape your presentation. Do they appreciate humor? Do they respond better to data? Are they easily overwhelmed? Adjusting your output (your emotions, what you say, what you write in an e-mail) can influence the results of others. You are therefore managing your own politics at work.

Common Bias

Any chance you've noticed the word choices I've used for the subjects? "Basic" emotions and "common" bias. They are used specifically because each section covers topics that you've heard. It can be said that the hardest thing about interacting with others is actually *working* with them in terms of your relationship with them. The more you can understand their viewpoint, the easier it will be for you to understand what they *need* or *want*—and you can help them on the way to completing your TEO action plan.

What is a bias? It's a predisposition to see or feel in a certain way based on some event or reason. It may not be logical—you may not even be able to explain it—but it's there. Common bias can come from a group of like-minded individuals who have worked together long enough to see others in a certain way (for example, the finance team seeing the marketing team as "the lazy ones").

Diversifying your team and understanding those biases in addition to recognizing the differences in emotions can help reduce conflict between you and others. Acknowledgement is always the first step, and while we might think we don't have any biases, they are part of human nature. By acknowledging this fact, we're able to reach a level of awareness to own up to our biases and attempt to remove them from our decision-making process. Then, leading by example, we can encourage others to feel comfortable in acknowledging their biases as well.

Before we talk about some of the biases that could affect your team and project, I want to share something that I've learned a few times—the hard way. *Perception is reality*. Sometimes it doesn't matter what you actually think or say—it's what others *hear* that matters. The more you can get in front of those perceptions, the more you can reduce conflict in your project and team.

THE BIAS LIST

Below is a list of some of the most commonly seen biases at work. For organizational and a bit of structural purposes, in the below list, two through five have been called decision-based biases, six through seven are known as attrition errors, and eight through nine are in a group called perception distortion (Robbins and Judge 2014).

For example, if we're talking about an e-commerce site like Amazon or eBay, perception is reality. If a page loads in two seconds, but the customer feels as if it loads in five seconds, it is the perception of five seconds that will be mentally logged by the customer, complained about, and considered by the tech team for solutions.

Here's the list of the bias or perception challenges you may see during your TEO project:

1. *Self-fulfilling bias, also known as the self-fulfilling prophecy.* It occurs when whatever you expect will happen, happens. Know you won't get that raise? You work at the level of mediocrity, and poof, you don't get the raise. Your performance expectations are set—whatever work you put into a task is equal to the expected work you get out.
   Counter it by getting perspective from others and taking a step back once in a while.

2. *Escalation of commitment.* You know the project is failing. Your team knows it's failing. But you've spent over 100 hours in the last month on it together, and you just can't stop now. This bias occurs when you decide to stay with a project, even when you have clear information to show that the project isn't working or that you're taking the wrong path. You are consciously deciding to follow a direction, even though more than likely it's the wrong one.
   Counter it by asking for a perspective from others and listening to them.

3. *Randomness error.* Things happen for a reason, right? You give your money to a financial investment company, and your advisor says he can beat the market because he can predict with a certain level of accuracy. He assures you that you will double your money in the next three years. Sure, he *may* be right, but you are taking a chance. This error occurs when you truly believe you can predict the results of what is really a series of random events. This bias can make some people feel more confident in their decisions—and more surprised when they don't work out.

Counter it by recognizing the different events that must correctly occur (such as the steps in your action plan), do a risk assessment to objectively weight different areas of the project, or take a step back and ask what you may feel overly confident about.

4. *Risk aversion.* Almost at the other end of the bias spectrum is risk aversion—or trying to avoid risks at all costs. People in this category will fight change simply because it's unknown, or would just prefer the sure bet versus going off the deep end with a risky result.

    Counter it in people averse to risk or change by helping them see the benefits of the TEO project (or that particular part of the action plan that affects them). Show them the results that you expect, and what you'll do if something happens (and preferably, that if something does go wrong, it won't be as bad as they think).

5. *Hindsight bias.* I like to call this one "the Monday morning quarterback." You turn on your favorite sports show the day after the big game only to find the announcers saying (sometimes smugly), "Yup, I expected Rodgers to throw the final touchdown and win the game." Hindsight bias is just that—falsely believing you have predicted the result of an outcome, after the event has occurred! Sounds too good to be true, right? Sometimes it is.

    Counter it by deciding how much of an impact this bias has on your project or action plan. If someone is there at every step saying "I told you so" every time you are wrong, you may want to have a discussion and ask for support in a different way. If someone is saying "I told you so" but in a supportive, even cheerleader way, then that's actually a good bias—and let them say it more!

6. *Fundamental attribution error (FAE).* FAE is believing that the reason something happened (mainly in a positive way) is more because of you (internal, personal reasons) and less because of other, external reasons (other support, outside help, things beyond your control). If you are seeing this error in your TEO project or day-to-day life, I'd recommend spending some time learning more beyond the short introduction here in this book.

    Counter it in a team member by finding out why the person believes that he or she contributed to the project's success more than others did. However, work on sharing perspective in a group environment where one person is not singled out.

7. *Self-serving bias.* Picture this: You've been helping your boss put together the perfect presentation for the executive team at your company. You created the beginning and middle, and he did some of the finishing touches. You brief your boss on the key points, where to drive the points home, and where to let the executives make their own decisions. The two of you go to the presentation, and he nails it—based largely because of what you did and how you helped him get there. When you come back to the office, he pats himself—not you—on the back. He says that he really has an eye for their needs, what they want, and how they pitched it. It's as if you never worked or even laid eyes on the project! This is an example of a self-serving bias—an

individual who thinks his or her success comes from his or her internal strengths and talents. Perhaps there is room for others in that success, perhaps not.

Counter it by taking strength in knowing you did a good job and seeking out others who can see it as well. You may never receive the feedback or appreciation you want from people who are completely wrapped in their own problems, so don't spend too much time trying. It may be worth the conflict to manage the politics at work to help the other side see your point of view—or it may be a better use of your time to find a new source of motivation. It's your call.

8. *Selective perception.* Selective perception can be a good thing—you're focusing on a particular item. What if you're only focusing only on the top 20 percent of your customers, but somehow (knowingly or not), you've ignored the next group that could be your new sweet spot? What if you're focused on your rising stars but ignoring the group that you know least about—the managers who are causing the most attrition? Note that this group includes people, objects, and events. As an example, think of the car or pet you have had. Chances are that whatever your car or pet—such as a gray Explorer or a blond terrier—you pay closer attention. There is nothing notable about either of those—but since you have more than common knowledge about those objects, there is an increased probability you will focus more on those items, people, or objects than others.

   Counter it by realizing that this bias happens to just about everyone. *Get perspective.* Ask others their perception. Take a step back—perhaps even use analytics to break you out of this bias.

9. *Halo effect.* Say that an average employee on your team did an outstanding job on her last project, which she finished one week before evaluations were due. The executive team complimented the project. However, the rest of the year, her performance was barely average. If you were to give that individual top marks based on her last project alone, you would be guilty of the halo effect—giving an evaluation or basing an opinion on a single characteristic instead of looking at the entire picture—in this case, the annual review based only on the last project. Think back to the last time you had to do an evaluation of another person. Perhaps you had the standard annual evaluation. How did you track all of the accomplishments the person had made the previous year? Was it easier or more difficult to remember the stuff from the beginning of the year—or the last two weeks? Typically, it's the last two weeks—and that leads to recency bias.

   Counter it by knowing it exists. Be aware of "the last great thing" you remember about people, projects, results. Realize that you could be focusing on events that may not have been that impactful in the grand scheme of a year. And (surprise!) get other viewpoints and perspectives.

BIAS PICTURE—TURNING INDIVIDUALS INTO TEAMS

A player who makes a team great is more valuable than a great player. Losing yourself in the group, for the good of the group, that's teamwork.

> —John Wooden, University of California, Los Angeles (UCLA),
> men's basketball coach who led the team to win the National
> Collegiate Athletic Association (NCAA) championship 10 times.

In this section, we turn to the group—and how it makes decisions. The quote above from John Wooden is a great one in that it talks about turning individuals into team players.

One of the more widely accepted "team structures" is Tuckman's stages of group development (named for Bruce Tuckman), which I like to call the "forming storming" team model (see Figure 9.1). There are five stages: forming, storming, norming, performing, and adjourning (Stein 2017). You may be putting together a new team or building on one already in place. Your action plan may require you to work across teams you've never worked with—or bring raw talent together in a new group. Almost all teams go through most of the stages listed, so if you are working on a team in the TEO project, you may find yourself in a few of these stages.

1. **Forming.** I'll call this the honeymoon phase. For the most part, team members want to be around you in this first stage, and either they are excited about the project or they don't know what to expect.

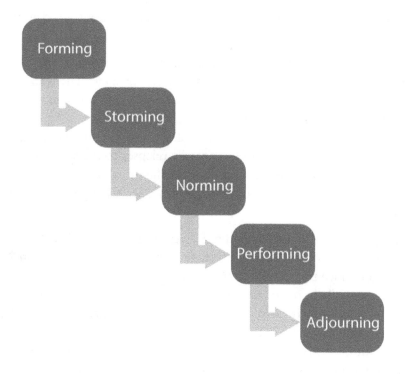

FIGURE 9.1.   Stages of Team Development

What you can do: Have a kickoff meeting to outline the action plan, including your goals and how you plan to reach them. Set up guidelines, goals, parameters, or guardrails. If you want to take it a step further, have each member talk about how they could best contribute to the team.

2. **Storming.** Ah, yes, now the fun begins. Just like in the dating world, the honeymoon phase is over, and you now see each other more clearly. You and others may not be able to do everything you said you would do, and the expectations you set for each other (and the project) may not be as high. Your perception about the expectations and the team may change as you start figuring out who the real team is.
    What you can do: Discuss your options—early. You may need to go back to the parameters you set up earlier and to focus on individual steps to accomplish. Everyone may need to take a step back (and a deep breath) and remember why you're doing what you're doing. (That's something you might want to define before undertaking any project or life endeavor—revisit the personal drive and intention.)

3. **Norming.** There was a song from the 1990s called "Back 2 Good" by Matchbox Twenty. That's where you are now. You've resolved the issues (mostly), and if you get far enough in this stage, you've set more reasonable and flexible norms and expectations (Stein 2017). Now that you know the team member to your right is not out to sabotage you (or the project), you may even be open to receiving constructive criticism (and to returning some as well).
    What you can do: You're moving past the storming stage. It's time to roll up your sleeves and do what you said you'd do. You may want to schedule regular check-ins to make sure everyone's on the same page. As in any relationship, communication is key.

4. **Performing.** Sometimes this stage blends with the last as some teams will transition to it quickly from resetting boundaries in the norming stage. The team members build on each other—their strengths and weaknesses—and move forward with how they can best accomplish what's left on the action plan list.
    What you can do: Keep on keeping on. If all goes well, you'll be in this stage the longest. Don't worry if your team temporarily relapses to the storming stage, requiring a return visit to the norming stage, but for the most part, the earlier stages are bumps in the road (and not roadblocks—if so, see Chapter 8 for additional support).

5. **Adjourning.** Some call this the "ending" stage. Others argue that the process needs just four stages and not an official fifth stage that ends the project (Stein 2017). I think it's a good idea to formally wrap up any major project that goes through a transition—especially in organizational-development work—to bring it to a close. Celebrate the successes. If the plan doesn't go well, for whatever reason, fail forward. Find out why it didn't work, and then try it a different way next time.
    What you can do: Make sure to complete this stage. People may drift off as their individual contributions end, but keep them (and yourself) engaged so

that everything that should get done, gets done. Don't forget to evaluate how you did personally and as a team (there will probably be a next time, right?). Finally—celebrate.

9.3 Activities and Application

When to Use Teams

Sometimes using teams for a project seems obvious. And sometimes having a team is overkill and leads to frustration and a slower work schedule and less productivity. Did you ever work on a team project in school and *know* that you could have done the project much better on your own, without all those nitwits? Well, there is a bit of truth to that.

It's also a matter of picking the right number of people at the table—not too few but also not so many that there's more talk than action.

If you have the choice—and you may with your TEO project—base your decision on whether to create a team on the size and makeup of your organization. If you work in a smaller company and lead a smaller group of people, it may be more obvious that you don't need a team to help you lead the project. You may just need some supporters, early adopters, or advocates.

The following questions can help you decide whether to use teams in your own project (Robbins and Judge 2014). My rule of thumb is that for every 20–25 people who are affected by the TEO project, you need one team member to help support you, field questions, evaluate the process, and push back when needed. You may find that a different formula works better for your team or organization.

Activity: When Not to Use Teams

Not every project requires a team to accomplish the mission. Before putting together your "ultimate team," ask yourself the following questions. If you answer no to at least one of the questions, you may want to reconsider the use of a team for your project:

Can one person more effectively do the work?

_____

_____

_____

_____

Does the work create a common goal or purpose?

_____

_____

_____

_____

Are the members of the group interdependent? Do they need each other's work to get their own work done?

_____

_____

_____

_____

_____

9.4 Real Stories

Backup Begins ... at the Beginning of a Question

I was in a meeting when the topic of communicating the equity partner buyout came up. As the HR member of the executive team, I knew that if the company did not put together a clearly stated message to employees, the employees would make up their own message. The employee-developed message would have been based on innuendo, partially overheard communications, and their anxiety. I shared my thoughts with the assembled team.

The president quickly shook his head in a "no" gesture. While I considered my reply, another member of the team agreed with me and added his perspective to the communication; next someone else said send it out as a short statement and a FAQ list. The VP of marketing volunteered to wordsmith a message—crisis averted.

I was surprised, and pleased, by this support. How did this happen anyway?

RELATIONSHIP AND BRIDGE BUILDING

I was new to the company role—less than a year. But during that time, I had spent many hours in the different leaders' offices getting to know them, talking with them about their ideas, thoughts, and how I might be of assistance to them. I let them share their comments about the company's history, its challenges, and their suggestions on how the company might improve. Needless to say, I had comments of agreement and when appropriate, I offered a different perspective. No, we did not solve the world's problems, but we did kick around a few ideas.

Whenever a leader asked for help or even implied that I could help with a certain point, I made it a priority and circled back to them in just a couple of days. I spent as much time as possible wandering around the office chatting with employees at their desks, the breakroom, or hallway. We used to call it "managing by wandering around." Maybe today it is "managing without texting." During the wanderings, I learned much and was able to share a substantial amount of the information with the respective leader. If the information was the least bit sensitive, I did ask employees if I could share the information with their boss. Employees almost always said yes.

Later in staff meetings, as appropriate and when the occasion would present itself, I would share an idea that one of the leaders may have mentioned in one of our discussions. Giving him credit, I would say something like "John, a few weeks ago we sort of kicked this topic around. Why don't you share your idea on XYZ?"

I was building positive, straight forward relationships with my peers and their teams. And at the same time, I was identifying gaps in the organization and helping the leaders fill those gaps. I was not asking for anything, but giving much instead. Through this process, I believe I gained the respect and trust of the team. They knew I was not out to make myself look good, but I wanted the entire team (company) to do well.

If you take a sincere interest in others, learn about them, their goals, desires, and needs, not only can you feel good about yourself, but when you least expect it, an ally will come to your rescue.

—Bill Crigger, President, Compass Career Management Solutions,
Compass & Strategic Partner Performance Culture

Building the Backups—Before You Even Hit the Work Floor

HR executives can often be perceived by their peers as having counterproductive ideas and requirements. Recently, I was working with an HR executive who was tasked with rolling out a new staffing plan and job categorization strategy to a group of 20 senior leaders who were certain to have their own ideas on the correct way to proceed.

The HR executive was very confident in her plans; however, she was very nervous about the presentation. Legally, the job categorization strategy was a requirement and not open to debate. The new staffing plan was a result of a shift in the CEO's financial philosophy. Although she didn't initiate these changes, the HR executive was responsible for creating and rolling out the solutions.

She started to walk me through her presentation, and I asked her to switch gears and walk me through the likely perspectives of the 20 senior leaders in the room. Right on cue she mentally went around the table and filled me in on all of the objections and interruptions she was certain she would get during her presentation. When she was finished, I said "perfect" and she looked confused.

We took every objection and interruption she thought she would get and wove them into her introduction. This allowed her to quickly defuse any confrontation, demonstrate a high level of situational awareness, and focus her presentation on the plans she was proud of.

As a result, she finished her 60-minute presentation with only one interruption, which she handled by referencing her introduction. She received overwhelming buy-in from the majority of the senior leadership team, and the CEO ended the meeting by stating "So it's done. We roll this out to our teams Monday."

—Michael Reddington, CFI, Vice President of Executive Education,
Wicklander-Zulawski and Associates

The Backup That Can Only Come from a Coffee Cup

BACKGROUND

As the chief engineer on a US Navy frigate, I was assigned to join the ship overseas and assumed my new position with the ship in the Mediterranean. The units assigned to this group included ships from the United States, United Kingdom, Portugal, Spain, the Netherlands, and Canada. The department I led consisted of about 65 sailors including four other officers and about seven senior enlisted leaders. To say that the crew was put through the paces was an understatement. We worked hard, conducted exercises, and supported the crew with water, propulsion, electrical power, sanitary services, damage control, and repair facilities. Our watch routine was a typical three-section rotation (staying overnight every third night) with watches of four to six hours. It was, in all respects, a normal deployment. However, the ship faced a critical engineering inspection after the deployment (five months from the day I joined the ship).

WHAT I PERCEIVED

The engineering inspection was a real concern to me. The road to a successful career in the Navy was littered with the careers of engineers who had failed these inspections. And, since timing was critical, having the inspection at the end of the deployment was good in the sense that the operators were going to be well-seasoned, but keeping the equipment fully operational after six months of constant use was a challenge. Indeed, when I took over as the chief engineer, I was confronted with the news that the ship did not have the basic level of acceptable equipment and was operating on waivers from higher authority. I believed that the very nature of working hard and meeting missions within our team was earning a reputation as a great ship and crew but was ultimately setting the department (and the ship's reputation) on a path for failure.

WHAT HAPPENED

Despite every best effort to keep things going, equipment kept breaking, people were getting hurt, and the demands on the crew to meet the operational commander's requirements increased. We approached the end of deployment with a combination of pride in accomplishment but an increasing level of risk. As the deployment wound down and the focus shifted toward the inspection, a catastrophic failure to one of the ship's diesel generators occurred. This meant that our ship had gone below the level of acceptable minimal equipment and was at a very high level for failure. To say that I was upset and frustrated with the situation is an understatement. I was convinced that my career was in real jeopardy. And it showed.

CRITICAL BACKUP ARRIVED

I was just coming off watch and heading to get a cup of coffee and a bite to eat on the mess deck. While I was pouring my coffee, I was paged over the ship's general announcing system, and my presence was requested in the major engineering space. When I arrived in the main engine room, the watch team told me about another casualty. I got up to speed, gave some orders, sank deeper into a depressed state, and returned to the mess deck for that cup of coffee.

When I got there, the senior enlisted leader in my department was waiting for me. He took my cup of coffee, poured it into the sink, and escorted me to the chief petty officer's mess. When the door opened, two other senior enlisted leaders were waiting.

Resting on the table was a coffee cup, personalized with my name and my warfare specialty. I sat down in front of the cup, now brimming with warm coffee. My coffee cup was refilled multiple times and I began to feel as though I could relax. The discussion went on to multiple topics, but not the engineering problems.

When the senior enlisted chief and I had the room alone, he told me that equipment was going to break and that the emotional attachment to my job was good, but it could be taken to the extreme. He said that I had to focus on the important things like family, baseball, and education. He assured me that we would not get all the equipment fixed, and he further assured me that the crew would make every effort to do well on the test. And then he told me I needed to rest and that deep sleep was needed. I left the chief's mess, took a shower, and climbed into my rack.

Eight hours later I awoke with a shifted perspective; I began to understand that the most important thing I could do would be to lead my team and do the best job I could in spite of my concerns. The backup team (perhaps it was the coffee) allowed me to see things from a different vantage point; I began focusing on the larger picture and shifted a lot of responsibility to the senior enlisted leadership who were more than capable of meeting the rigors of a tight schedule.

Even though nothing had changed (the crew was overworked, equipment kept breaking, and the operational schedule remained challenging), everything came into a new light. I was more confident because I felt like I had someone backing me up. I felt as if I was able to clearly see a way forward and not focus on the potential of a negative inspection. I also realized that I was not alone.

The Final Result

We, in fact, had a difficult inspection but we were able to meet minimal equipment and we blew the operational portion out of the water. During our final inspection presentation, I took the final out-brief sitting alongside my commanding officer and drinking from a most impressive personalized coffee mug.

—D.P. "Skip" Shaw, Captain, US Navy, Retired

Sometimes Your Backup Is Saying Nothing at All

When I was in boot camp, my gunnery sergeant called me into his office one afternoon. For some reason, I tended to get called into his office a lot (which was not really a good thing)—and he was always giving me some advice on something, or telling me how I had done something else wrong (mostly the latter). In this one incident, about halfway through boot camp, he didn't talk. He asked me why I was there, where I planned on going in the military, and what brought me to this point (in boot camp).

Surprised, I started talking about the reasons I joined the Navy, what I wanted to do (lead people, do something different, do something for my country)—and continued with a variety of information. I talked for probably 15 minutes, and probably could have gone for more if we hadn't had a deadline for a meeting in another 5 minutes.

He pointed out his original question. Had I answered his question? Yes. But did I go beyond it? Did I keep talking and tell him a lot more than he asked for and give him more information—not only about the background to the question but about who I was and what I stood for? Absolutely.

He taught me an extremely important lesson that day, and it remains one of my top five leadership rules that I live by. If you're the boss, you don't have to talk all the time. In fact, it's better that you talk the *least* and get your people to talk more. Ask questions of them. Listen to their answers. People like to share what they know—they want to tell you how to solve a problem or just talk about themselves. Give them the chance. It will make you a better leader—for your own sake, as well as theirs!

—*Ashley Prisant Lesko*

SECTION 5

Crossing the Finish Line Is Only the Beginning (Knowing "When")

CHAPTER 10
Kaizen for Life

10.1 The SBSG Story

Elizabeth takes a step back and surveys the room. Eight people are present—her boss, two people from customer service (CS), two people from operations (from different areas), two directors from different departments, and Elizabeth herself. One of the directors is a guest, and her boss is the "stakeholder."

SBSG is holding its first kaizen activity. This part is not so unusual—many industries have been trying them out for years. What makes this one different? This kaizen would be nontraditional. It would be on a *nonoperations* process (as Elizabeth understands it, kaizen typically improves multistep processes, functions, or departments—not offices).

Elizabeth has heard a few things about kaizen from the process improvement team— the "lean team," as they are called. She has heard that you could also use kaizen on non-operations processes such as office work as long as a process needs to be improved.

Her TEO project is going well, but in one area, CS, she is struggling to find a solution. The results of the assessment and the next steps in her action plan call for giving the CS team members more time away from the phone so they can do more of what they want (in various areas, depending on the person). But when they tried to implement TEO in CS, they found that the team members did not have enough time on the phone and that their customer service scores slipped if they weren't right next to their phone or e-mail.

She decides to try kaizen to find out if there is some other, perhaps crazy, perhaps revolutionary, way to make the process go faster—and implement TEO at the same time.

10.2 The Nuts and Bolts

OK, raise your hand if you know what kaizen (KI-zen) is *and* can define it.

Chances are about 50/50 that you've heard of the word. If you're in the operations field or attached to a process-oriented company, chances are even greater you could give a definition and maybe even share an example.

Several definitions of kaizen exist. They come from industry, corporate, and academic alike. One definition is from the world of business:

"Business philosophy or system that is based on making positive changes on a regular basis, as to improve productivity" (Dictionary.com).

A closer-to-home version is this:

"An approach to one's personal or social life that focuses on continuous improvement" (Dictionary.com).

On the other hand, an industry definition for kaizen may be "a strategy where employees at all levels of a company work together proactively to achieve regular, incremental improvements to the manufacturing process. In a sense, it combines the collective talents within a company to create a powerful engine for improvement" (Vorne 2016). Kaizen, if understood and used wisely, can make incremental improvements to an organization that can save thousands of dollars (yep, you read those words correctly). Got your attention yet?

Improvement. Continuous. Proactive. Incremental. These words are typically paired with kaizen. Using the kaizen strategy, a process is reviewed from multiple viewpoints—perhaps from people who aren't even familiar with the work or task itself. The process is broken down in pieces and then rebuilt in a way that is more conducive to work, more efficient or effective, or better overall for the company.

Isn't that what you're trying to do with the talent engagement optimization of your company?

You're trying to drive change—but not by small hacks. You're changing processes and systems that have been in place for perhaps a long period of time. You're looking to make enhancements to the foundation and structure of talent engagement in your organization. This is a part of making positive changes by continuing the cycle of testing, learning, and implementing—hence, kaizen.

Would You Like an Example?

Think about something you do often. Perhaps you're an accountant with a month-end process that seems to never end because you have to wait for four people to complete their work before you can do yours. Perhaps you are an HR analyst who must perform manual data entry for each new employee, which takes an hour per individual (and your company hires at least 50 people a month).

The steps involved in the example tasks are forms of waste—which you can learn more about in Part 3 of this chapter, as well as in Appendix A, "The Seven Deadly Sins of Kaizen—the Seven Wastes." Think about all the steps that you take to accomplish a task. Could you do it better? Faster? Do you know that you could do it better but don't have the time to figure out how?

Kaizen means implementing change to help you *proactively* improve the process so that you are saving time before actually doing the work (or before you spend any more time on it), and it helps you *continually improve* to make the process faster and more efficient—so you can get to the things that really matter (and matter to you!).

My Project Is about TEO—Helping People Go Beyond the Job Description. Why Should I Care about Kaizen?

Kaizen is one of the best-kept secrets in operations! This is only partially true—in the last decade, more and more nontraditional operations industries (think restaurants and health care) have branched into time- and efficiency-saving tools—with kaizen being a main tool in their toolbox.

The goal of your project is optimization, making a process better—improving the situation. You want the process to be the best it can be. You also want the changes to stick. Kaizen can help you do this.

At this point, you may be eyeing the end of the project. The action plan steps are being crossed off, and you may even start seeing some results, some smiling faces, and some work done that has not been done before. You may have hit a roadblock or two (and if so, you've visited Chapter 8), but you're on your way—for the most part. Perhaps an area needs tweaking, and you're not sure how to fix it; perhaps you need a team to look at it. Kaizen can do that.

Kaizen can help when

- A team of different people can look at a problem and help you find a solution you may not have found on your own.
- You're almost finished but not sure the changes will last. How will the new changes work when you're not around? How do you know? What is the next process you will need to address or tackle?

Creating a Kaizen Culture

As we talked about in Chapter 2, change can be difficult for some, but once you've ripped off the bandage—disrupted people's lives in some fashion—you have the chance to make permanent (positive) changes: ones that are good for the company, your team, and you.

Some of you may already have a kaizen culture—or one that encourages continuous improvements in all areas of the job, quick failures ("fail forward"), and incremental movements of the needle—such as improving productivity by a few units, or saving five minutes every time the task is performed. For others, you may find people in the organization ready for a kaizen culture, but not sure how to move forward.

Let me first tell you how *not* to create a kaizen culture. In a former position, I was tasked with making improvements in my department. Sounds simple, right? So I learned about kaizen, dove into the process, figured out what was wrong (in my own mind), and then fixed it. Great, right? By the end of the week, I could boast great savings of 15 percent off 100 hours of work per week (yes, you can go ahead and promote me now, I am a rock star).

But my success was short-lived. The following Friday everything was back to the original way of working. A few people tried to follow the new process for about half a day the first day, but, after that, they quickly went back to doing things the old way. All my work, my data processing, my 15 percent savings … gone.

What happened? The new process was better. What was wrong with these people?

This is where I introduce the phrase "kaizen for life." I missed the boat on what the important people in the equation—the employees actually doing the work—wanted or needed. I essentially *told* them what to do, instead of working with them (as you should in kaizen) to find the best solution. Some of my processes were good, but I didn't have buy-in.

I've said it before, and I'll say it again: for changes, kaizen, or your action plan to work, *you must have buy-in.* You cannot implement systemic change without support from leadership. To create a successful large-scale change, you need the support from leadership to be the driving force of your value proposition.

Creating "kaizen for life" as part of the kaizen culture means creation of a follow-up process that checks in periodically to see if the changes are

- Effective.
- Still working.

A follow-up process enables you to hold in place the different parts of your action plan to make sure that your people actually benefit from using their strengths—or that their bosses are actually having one-on-ones with their staff, motivating as they should. What worked this year may not work next year. As turnover is an inherent part of an organization, team dynamics change as a result of people evolving in their respective career paths. Kaizen allows you to account for those inevitable changes within an organization and implement a strategy to keep up with the fast pace.

Your TEO does not end when you finish this book. It, just like everything else, is a continuous improvement. To make your TEO project stick, you must build a "holding in place" procedure to keep it going—even after the project ends and you move on to greater things.

Final Kaizen Notes

This chapter does not pretend to teach you everything about kaizen or how to carry out a kaizen strategy. The *idea* of kaizen is continuous improvement through incremental changes.

Key points:

- *Have references.* A recommended starting list is the References at the end of this book to help you if you'd like to dig more into the details. If you want more details, you can visit squarepegsolutions.org for help running a full kaizen process.
- *Know what you want.* Kaizen is a powerful tool, but it is not the answer to everything. Focus your efforts on a specific area or metric to maximize your goal or reward.
- *Use of a kaizen even if you're not in operations.* In fact, I'd challenge you to find an area in which you can't use kaizen. Go on. Try it.
- *Ask for help.* I've done lots of these projects for all industries—call in someone to help if you don't have the time or if you need perspective!

10.3 Activities and Application

We could devote an entire book to how to implement a kaizen process, but since the purpose of this chapter is "kaizen for life"—learning how to keep it going after the project has ended—we will focus briefly on how to use kaizen and then talk about a key component: the seven wastes.

Kaizen Steps

1. **Define your goal.** What do you want to accomplish? This should be a simple one- or two-liner: "reduce time spent in this process by 10 percent" or "improve communication between teams by 50 percent." You'll need to define how to measure that goal. (For example, how do you measure improved communication? I would do it based on e-mails sent or a survey response.) What's the goal for your kaizen strategy? (You can list more than one kaizen idea and more than one goal; however, there should be a primary goal for each kaizen idea.)

_____

_____

_____

_____

_____

_____

2. **Define the boundaries.** Where does the process or project start and stop? This is key; defining the boundaries is one of the most overlooked areas. Scope creep is where boundaries are set for a project and then events in the project such as "adding this would look good" or "doing that also would help the situation" make the project even bigger. You'll need to set the boundaries of the lane you're in. (For example, I did one project where our boundaries were the month-end process only for Tuesday through Thursday, the fourth week of the month, and 10 specific accounts. Anything outside of that we called "out of boundary.") If a solution comes up that is outside your set parameters, put it in the "parking lot"—an area set aside for good ideas that are to be tabled for a later time frame or project.

  What are the boundaries for your kaizen process?

_____

_____

_____

_____

_____

_____

3. **Pick the team.** The more diversity in terms of viewpoints and experiences—the better! You probably don't need to be told how important this step is—or how important it is to get the right people on your team. In this case, the right people are *different*. You may have one or two people from the department in which the process will be improved, but you may also have people—senior and junior alike—from completely different departments.

   A good rule of thumb is to have four to six people total, with one designated as the leader. You will also benefit from having a kaizen sponsor—a senior person in the company who is not part of the day-to-day actions but who will support and represent the team's results within the senior team.

   Who will be on your team?

   Kaizen leader _____

   Member 1 _____

   Member 2 _____

   Member 3 _____

   Member 4 _____

   Member 5 (optional) _____

   Member 6 (optional) _____

   Kaizen sponsor/stakeholder _____

4. **Designate the timeline.** Is this a small project? If so, you may need only a day or two, and only a one- to three-person team. A typical kaizen process lasts about a week (see Table 10.1). Set up the timeline so the team understands the time frame to work. It is said that people will work like the Boyle's gas law, meaning they will fill the space they are given. So, if you give them five days, they will take five days, but if you give them three, they'll finish their work in that time frame. Estimate the size of the project and go from that.

   As a guideline, here is the schedule for a typical five-day kaizen process:

   a. **Day 1.** Set up a team, establish team roles, observe the problem or process, and map out the process to understand each step—how long it takes, why it's necessary. Ask for employee feedback (from employees being impacted), report out.

   b. **Day 2.** Continue observing the problem and asking for employee feedback, talk over potential solutions, break the process (find new ways to try the process, find what makes it work, what makes it break down, etc.), report out.

   c. **Day 3.** Continue breaking the process as described in Day 2 and asking for employee feedback, run potential solutions, report out.

   d. **Day 4.** Continue running potential solutions, narrow to best solution, begin evaluation, report out.

   e. **Day 5.** Perform the final team evaluation, present the work to the executive team.

TABLE 10.1.   Your Timeline Plan for the Kaizen

	DAY	TIMELINE, STEPS, ACTION PLAN	DAILY GOAL
	Example	Initial meeting (30 minutes), set up teams (1 hour), walk the process (2 hours), brainstorm ideas (1 hour), timing of processes (2 hours), set up for day two (2 hours)	Prep for day two, have value stream map developed, ready for testing new ideas day two
1	Monday		
2	Tuesday		
3	Wednesday		
4	Thursday		
5	Friday		

Additional Notes:

_____

_____

_____

_____

_____

_____

_____

5. **Let them go.** Give team members their boundaries and expectations (including to report out) and get out of the way. You don't need to be with them every minute (unless you're on the team!). Go for it—let them run, and see what happens. How you will check in with them:

_____

_____

_____

_____

_____

_____

_____

6. **Kaizen follow-ups.** As I've mentioned earlier (and learned the hard way!), following up may be the most important step. Below is a suggestion of how to follow up—you may have more or less time based on your work.

a. **Week 2.** One person, typically the team leader, or assistant leader, spends 25–50 percent of his or her week with the process, touching base to ensure that the process sticks and intervening on any issues to help resolve them immediately.

b. **Week 3.** One person spends 5–10 percent of his or her week with the process, continuing to touch base.

c. **Week 4 and beyond.** One person spends a few minutes per week answering any questions as needed to ensure success in program.

Your kaizen follow-up program will look like:

_____

_____

_____

_____

_____

_____

_____

_____

_____

_____

_____

10.4 Real Stories

Led by Employees: Saving Time and Making It Safe for All

The example I am sharing took place in a fulfillment center. A fulfillment center is a modern packing warehouse that enables e-commerce companies to get away from having the necessary physical space to store all products. This is beneficial for merchants who need not have a physical store presence and need to sell and ship products to consumers.

Working at a fulfillment center is hard and can take a toll on the workers' physical health. One such example is at the packing station where fulfillment workers (or associates, as they were called) packed products in relevant cardboard cartons to ship them out to customers. If the cartons were too big or small, they had to redo the process. Often, they had to stuff excess packing materials in the large cartons to ensure that the products did not move excessively in the cartons when shipped. This resulted in extra non-value-added steps [author note: also known as waste—see Appendix A] for the associates and often resulted in safety incidents for associates, not to mention extra costs from using more packaging materials.

The leadership team decided to conduct a process improvement for this area using kaizens to improve the safety record in this space. We formed a team consisting of associates from the packing area, a quality manager, and associates from other departments to provide an outside perspective. We assigned a leader to the team—she was the manager of the packing area, and the expectation was that she would lead the efforts to roll this out across all shifts and to the rest of her peers in the packing area when the kaizen was completed.

The team spent time observing the packing process, collecting inputs from the associates, identifying discrete steps, and conducting time studies for each of these steps. They then stepped back and assessed and quantified their observations including what worked well in addition to any gaps in the process. For closing each gap, they came up with a goal (some based on data and some aspirational). For these stretch goals, the kaizen team working with inputs from the rest of the packing department came up with new processes.

The next steps were to try out the recommended processes and see if they indeed moved the needle on the goals. While some did, the rest did not. The team would regroup to see what did not work on their tests. Through these continuous testing and feedback cycles, the team made progress within a week on their goals. At the end of two weeks, the team concluded the kaizen and shared their observations and recommendations to leadership. The kaizen was successful as it identified at least five nonvalue steps that caused higher touch points and extra movements for the associates. The kaizen team recommended splitting items into small, medium, and large packing lines, introduced new packing box sizes in line with these sizes, and reduced the touch points and movements by 30 percent.

The recommendations were implemented and the team saw a reduction in injury by 40 percent, an improvement in efficiency by 30 percent, and a reduction in costs from excess packing material by 11 percent. The kaizen was a big success as it was primarily led by associates and for associates with the aim to improve safety.

—Karthik Sivakumar, Senior Director,
Product Management and Strategy

Starting Small with Kaizen—with Big Impact

They say that the first step is always the hardest. This adage could not be more fitting of my experience. When I was asked to rise above my station to lead a team of my co-workers and superiors in a kaizen burst event, the task was daunting and exciting! I knew what needed to be done, but I had no idea where to get started. Organizing a typical improvement project with typical meetings can be challenging enough, but a three-hour kaizen microburst? [Author note: A kaizen microburst is an extremely shortened kaizen for groups that may not have as much time available together, or who may adjust their schedule to work on their kaizen in short "bursts."]

I was reminded of something that a teacher once told me, "It doesn't matter where you start, so long as you get started," and with that in mind, I did. Once I got going, structuring the initial three-hour burst became easy. I knew my team, considered their strengths, their weaknesses, and how I could draw each of them out to become fully engaged. I made sure that the team changed location, activities, or simply their style of interaction regularly, to keep the meeting feeling fresh and new. The kickoff to the event was wildly successful; from there I only had to keep the momentum rolling.

To ensure that things continued to move, I relied on being highly organized. By providing my team with meeting agendas several days in advance, circulating post meeting notes to solidify expectations and accountability, and by getting in as much face time as possible, my team was informed, motivated, and engaged. In the end, we not only reached all of our project goals, we flew past them!

Reflecting now, on everything that transpired over the life of the project, I can say that I am proud of my team. Of their dedication and their willingness to trust and follow me as a leader. In future implementations, I will look back on this experience and remember the words of my teacher when I am feeling unsure of myself or how to begin, "It doesn't matter where you start, so long as you get started."

—*Stephen Shingara*

Kaizen: Bringing the Team Together

Kaizen, which means "continual improvement" in Japanese, is a mindset, a toolkit, and a way of improving your operations. It means always finding a better way of doing things, trying it out, iterating, and then finally implementing it. One key component of kaizen is frontline employee engagement in idea generation as well as implementing improvement projects.

As the head of a distribution center for a large e-commerce company, I had firsthand experience of how effective and powerful kaizen can be. The cycle time of our core process that directly impacted our customer was unacceptably long—more than 20 days in some cases. As a team, we gave ourselves a challenge to bring it down to less than five days! This seemed impossible at first.

We put together a strong kaizen team comprising our frontline associates and subject matter experts. We then mapped every step of the process in a giant process map by doing the work as a group. Once the process was mapped, we stepped back and observed the process being done by others while taking detailed notes on inefficiencies (the seven wastes) in the process.

Armed with this knowledge, we examined and measured each step in the process to identify how long it took, how much labor it required, and most importantly, did it add value for customers (will the customer pay for it?). That resulted in a detailed value-stream map of the process with clear areas of improvements. Leveraging the majority of our frontline associates, we pulled in creative and out-of-the-box ideas to solve these challenges.

Finally, utilizing standard automation, software, and lean and six sigma methodologies, the team systematically eliminated as many areas of inefficiency, defect, and waste as possible. While we didn't hit our initial goal of five days, the team did improve it to seven days—which was still a massive achievement. Because of the great work done by the team, we won the annual North American Process Improvement award, beating out more than 40 other challengers.

—*Ritesh Chaturbedi*

CHAPTER 11

Measuring Success

11.1 The SBSG Story

It is time. Elizabeth almost doesn't want to press Enter on the cell in her Excel sheet, because she is afraid of what the formula will say—or what the output of her nearly four months of progress with SBSG will be. She never thought that something that appeared so challenging at the onset would be easy to put together. It was the people—helping them understand that this improvement was actually *for them*, for a change—that made it harder.

   She thinks back to those early days. She had decided (and convinced her stakeholders) that the 10 percent productivity improvement would be the primary metric to measure the success of the TEO. So, she had conducted a short survey of employees in all departments taking part in the TEO project to determine how many hours they felt they spent on such things as

- E-mails.
- Meetings.
- Training.
- Actual job-description work.
- Breaks.
- Talking to peers.
- Free/open time (to be used productively at the employee's discretion).
- Wasted time (explanation required).
- Other (explanation required).

Included on the survey was a question asking participants to estimate, on a sliding scale, the percentage of their day they believed they spent on real work—in essence, how productive they thought they were each day. Last week, Elizabeth asked the same employees to complete the survey again to measure the differences between results pre- and post-TEO.

She also added a few more questions from the managers—what they perceived these were for their teams (both before and after).

Her goal is to see where the changes are and to find out if overall productivity has improved.

She presses Enter to run the formula. 12.43 percent comes up. She calculates the numbers again, in a different way just to be sure: 12.43 percent. Her goal had been 10 percent.

She did it.

11.2 The Nuts and Bolts

If you're one of those people who like to find out how a book ends to settle your curiosity, there could be a chance that you've jumped to this chapter, ready to understand the success of this program.

Spoiler alert—you'll need to go back a few chapters to see if you've actually been successful. It's basic math. How can you be successful in areas in which you don't have a measure of success?

Looking back: Section 1 discussed what you need to get started—how to measure success and how to create a baseline. Chapter 1 explored the concept of what you need to understand with that baseline, especially to get executive buy-in (for the cost, budget, and support of the program).

At this point, it is presumed that you've traveled along the course of the assessments, dug in, and found trends within your team, the individual employees, the culture, and the organization. You decided on productivity, strengths, leadership, communication, or another metric to determine the area of talent you wanted to engage and grow.

Reaching the end of the program was not enough, however, and you made sure to check on the progress of your program in Chapter 7 to make sure that you were on track. If you were veering off, you either adjusted or reset your course, depending on the need and flexibility of the program.

Congratulations on making it this far! The process probably hasn't been easy, and you may have met resistance along the way. It's time to assess where you and the program are, and where to go from here.

A few examples in this chapter show how to analyze the before and after, but in general, there are two main ways to compare results: quantitatively and qualitatively. For more information and references on how to look at quantitative and qualitative data, please check Chapter 4.

Quantitative Results—It's in the Numbers

Quantitative work is defined in terms of numbers and statistics. It can give us a reference to measure performance, set up a dashboard of metrics, and see how you are doing in comparison in terms of time, money, or other relative numbers (Berman 2014).

There are a few ways to use quantitative data, and, as this book is not a deep dive into numbers and data, we'll keep to the high level and point you in a few directions. (If you want to dig further, search the Internet for a term like "simple quantitative analysis" or "example quantitative analysis.")

MEANS, MEDIANS, AND MODES

You can average numbers in different ways and they can help you with a lot of your data. If you have collected survey scores, you will probably go with the mean (average of all numbers, with equal weight). You can compare the before and after of a benchmark using the mean. For example, say that you measured the work engagement score of a department of 20, and the before number was 3.4. After the change or implementation, you calculate the score again, and it is now 4.4—a difference of a 1.0 and a nearly 30 percent improvement, $(4.4–3.4)/3.4 = 0.294$ or 29.4 percent.

STATISTICAL DATA

There are many methods for analyzing information at a higher level—for instance, calculating the frequency, the variance of data, where the numbers are dispersed or concentrated, or which people are in the 25th percentile. Software such as SPSS can help deliver these numbers, but a spreadsheet program like Excel can also do much of the heavy lifting these days. If you go either of these routes, you can watch YouTube videos and use other methods to learn how to input the numbers properly and how to read the results!

Qualitative Results—Interpretation Is Key

When I first started learning about qualitative data, I thought you really had to "qualify" the data since there were really no numbers—the analysis was all left to interpretation. Although my mental model or viewpoint was a little off, there is some truth in the ability to simplify words and paragraphs into information that can be used.

For example, say you interviewed five people at the beginning of the project, and now you've interviewed those same people at the end. You ask essentially the same questions and now have the results in front of you. How do you interpret them?

WHO SHOULD INTERPRET THE DATA?

If you did the interviews both times—and for best results, you should have—then you should interpret the data. Would someone else interpret the data differently? Probably. Would that affect the results of the data? Not necessarily, but keep reading.

Although some may find this explanation trivial, qualitative analysis (understanding the data) is about reviewing, understanding, and reading the trends—and then relating the results in a way to help others understand what the information is telling you—with supporting points (such as specific comments or trending words) showing how the information resulted in the analysis you have.

At the end of the data collection, the qualitative data will paint a story that explains (in words) what has happened. For example, while evaluating new managers and frontline managers, I interviewed the employees who reported to them. When I reviewed the notes from these interviews, I realized that the employees used these three terms to describe what they wanted their manager to be better at: "communication," "feedback," and "training." Here are five traditional approaches to qualitative analysis (Creswell 2012):

- **Narrative.** Explaining a sequence of events, perhaps by using a story in the summary as an explanation.
- **Grounded theory.** Using the actual words as information points, recognizing trends, and creating results based on a known theory (such as workplace engagement or extrinsic motivation).
- **Case study.** Explaining a situation through a story using a company or event to relate the data. Case studies are one of the primary tools for teaching students in business school.
- **Ethnography.** Immersing yourself in an environment and reporting on the results.
- **Phenomenological.** Using the words that are given to describe an event, story, or phenomenon.

Using the key leadership trends and data that I had analyzed (building on "communication, feedback, and training") I was able to make recommendations to clients. For example, several clients wanted to develop their managers but did not have time to create a full leadership program because their HR department was small or they had no training team set aside. My recommendations helped them focus on developing their managers quickly in the top three areas.

In the Part 3 of this chapter, we will talk about ways you can use your qualitative evaluation in 360-degree reviews and in analyzing the trends. One of the challenges with qualitative evaluation is that it can be more time-consuming than its quantitative brother (assuming that you know what you're doing in both areas already!), but it can be equally as rewarding given that it can tell a story, which may help bring senior leaders around to understanding the situation.

A note of caution: Qualitative data can be looked on as the weaker of the two in analysis—for some executives (especially in hard data areas, such as engineering, operations, and IT), stories are not enough to move them to spend money. In this case, you may need to present qualitative data in combination with quantitative; the stories and numbers can together provide a compelling analysis.

My personal viewpoint? I think both quantitative and qualitative data have their place in business as a way to share results and the success of projects. It depends on your company's culture, its acceptance of new or different data, and what is needed for the organization to deem a project a success. You may need to make a judgment call.

I'VE GOT THE RESULTS. NOW WHAT?

Excellent. You may want to jump ahead to Chapter 12, which will show you how best to use the results to get buy-in again and how to present the data in a meaningful way to executives—taking into account their perspective, their needs, and the drivers for continuing the talent engagement project.

WHAT IF I DON'T HAVE THE RESULTS?

Don't panic. You've invested time. You've probably invested a lot of time, perhaps some money, and a fair amount of talent. You may even feel that you've invested some of your reputation on this initiative.

WHAT DO I HAVE TO SHOW FOR IT AT THIS POINT?

You went through the motions, you measured twice and cut once, and now you're at the end of the project—or what you thought was the end of the project. But you're not where you thought you'd be.

This realization can lead to two concerns: What if you calculated the results, but you either didn't get the results at all—no trends or informational points that seem to make sense—or didn't get results you wanted?

THE PROJECT'S DONE AND I DIDN'T GET THE RESULTS. AT ALL.

OK, let's not hyperventilate yet. You just need to figure out where you are in the process.

First, what were you trying to measure (for example, engagement, productivity, communication skills)?

_____

_____

_____

_____

_____

_____

_____

_____

How were you trying to measure it?

_____

_____

_____

_____

_____

_____

_____

_____

Take a look at Part 3 of this chapter. If the metric that you would like to measure is in the list, you can use the example to see where you could compare your data. If you feel you didn't get good information to start—and you know there's results—think about working on a qualitative review such as a 360-degree assessment, explained below.

Chances are you were expecting this project to turn at least a little south, given that you assessed the program as you went along (see Chapter 7). However, if the results caught you by surprise, you have two options:

1. Continue reading this chapter.
2. Revisit Section 1 (about the best way to succeed in this book) and Chapter 2. Your plan may be a fairly innovative idea for the company or department, and it may take a few attempts to achieve the results you know are possible.

THE PROJECT'S DONE AND I DIDN'T GET THE RESULTS I WANTED

Change takes time. If you have followed the plan to a T, you have been working on this program for only 100 days. There could be many reasons you aren't there yet, you're not quite getting the results you want—or you got some that you may have realized, and some that may not be so obvious:

*   Not enough time.
*   Lack of executive support.
*   Lack of direct manager support.
*   Lack of team/individual support.
*   Too many competing projects.
*   You didn't get a good benchmark before.
*   The TEO plan worked, but it just didn't get as far as you wanted.
*   Lack of buy-in on concepts—how the results were achieved, the methods you used.

Take a breath and a moment to think about it. What were the areas that may have prevented you from getting the results you had hoped for?

_____

_____

_____

_____

_____

_____

Feel free to go back to Chapter 8, "Roadblocks," to help you evaluate what stopped you and at what point.

If you've made it this far, and you've seen results, congratulations. Even if they are not as great as you wanted, the results can take time. People on your team or in your department or company may not have experience with a change of this nature. Change is hard for some (see Chapter 2 to understand why, and Chapter 8 for additional support), and it may take a few iterations for everyone to accept the new way of operating.

Work on understanding the five *W*s of the situation:

*   Why didn't the results go as far as you expected?
*   Where was the holdup; what held the project back?
*   What were the fundamental ideas that you had that did not get carried out?
*   Who do you need to work with to move the needle forward from here?
*   What will you do differently next time?

Answers:

_____

_____

_____

_____

_____

_____

_____

_____

_____

_____

_____

11.3 Activities and Application

Let's get started. What were the metrics that you used in benchmarking? Check out Section 1 (on how to know if you're successful), and list the metrics that you benchmarked. Use Tables 11.1 and 11.2.

TABLE 11.1.   Quantitative Metrics

ITEM #	ITEM	BEFORE (SEE SECTION 1, PART 5)	AFTER (MEASURED HERE)	PERCENTAGE INCREASE/ DECREASE	COMMENTS
Ex.	Work Engagement Score	3.4	4.3	29.4%	
1					
2					
3					
4					
5					

TABLE 11.2.   Qualitative Metrics

ITEM #	ITEM	TRENDS—BEFORE (SEE SECTION 1, PART 5)	AFTER (MEASURED HERE)	COMMENTS/IMPACT
Ex.	Development of Leaders	No support from leaders, no communication, employee feeling ignored	Seeing awareness, trying to reach out, having one-on-ones at least monthly, visible engagement	Need to expand leader training to other departments, productivity increasing with ideas generated
1				
2				
3				
4				
5				

If you're not ready to fill out the table yet, that's fine. Let's go through some examples to see if they help clarify how to measure the success of your program.

Application

STORY 1: GROWTH STOPS, THEN GETS BACK ON TRACK

Background: ABC Tech Company (ABC TechCo) has been growing for 10 years but then stopped. For over five years, the company had stayed at the same level, at the same number of people, and basically the same level of revenue. The HR manager of ABC TechCo wanted to understand from an employee perspective how to engage and motivate the employees and to encourage them to suggest ways to help the company innovate.

Metrics used: Utrecht Work Engagement Scale (UWES), interviews, 360-degree reviews, communication skills

Benchmarking (how the results were evaluated): Completed the UWES at the beginning of the program, after each month, and at the end; conducted interviews at the beginning and the end of the program

Time/duration of project: Six months from beginning to end

Analysis and example:

1. **Quantitative.** With the UWES scores, the HR manager evaluated the teams—as a group and as a company. She looked at the individual scores (vigor, dedication, absorption) to see how they changed over each month.

a. One month, she found a drop in dedication by a significant amount (about 20 percent), so she asked the VP of the department for a possible explanation. He told her that a rollout had occurred in the department.

b. The results of this survey showed that something had not gone as the VP had planned. In further interviews, the HR manager found that the communication of the rollout was missing several pieces, and many people had assumed the worst about the program.

c. The VP recommunicated the plan, explained it in detail, and allowed for a 30-minute Q&A of the new rollout.

d. The next month, the overall score for that department was 10 percent higher than the results two months earlier.

2. **Qualitative.** The HR manager entered the main comments from the interviews into an Excel sheet and listed the name of the person, the department, the title (for example, accountant), and any comment in the first four columns. Initially, she left the fifth column blank but later titled it "Summary" (see Table 11.3).

a. She begin pulling keywords out of the comments such as "lack of communication," "lack of innovation," or "don't see career advancement."

b. She compiled short summaries, longer phrases, complete sentences and partial paragraphs of the statements like this throughout the rest of the document and labeled it in the fifth column as "Summary."

c. After writing the summaries, she sorted based on the fifth column—"Summary"—and then sorted the comments into trends.

d. From there, she was able to determine the most important areas of focus for the employees in the interviews.

TABLE 11.3.   Story 1—Growth Stops, then Gets Back on Track

NAME	DEPARTMENT	TITLE	COMMENTS	SUMMARY
Wendy	Finance	Accounting	I never feel like my manager tells me anything	Lack of communication

STORY 2: GETTING IT DONE

Background: XYZ Medical Services Company (XYZ Med) experienced high growth—an average of nearly 30–50 percent year over year for revenue in the last three years. Employee growth was even greater—from 20 employees the first year, to 80 the second—and the expectation is that the number will increase to over 250 in year three, maybe even 400 by the end of year four. The leaders of the company didn't want to see their culture—a blend of innovation, unique talents, and entrepreneurial creativity—be lost by the massive hiring they were doing. They also wanted to make sure they were hiring appropriately and were concerned that several of the more experienced employees (those who had been there the longest) were slowing in their work—leading to needing more people earlier than expected and potentially teaching their new hires bad habits.

XYZ Med had seen that one of the largest-growing areas was in its financial and accounting departments. The company had been hiring in those departments at a much higher rate than anywhere else, a non-value-added item (a task that was not needed and essentially wasted time) toward the actual customer. Leaders were concerned about reports that the employees in those areas were not working as hard as employees in other departments, resulting in greater hiring in those areas. They asked the training manager to assess the overall situation.

Metrics used: Productivity, leadership development, talent engagement, entrepreneurial creativity (unique to the company, self-generated measurement)

Benchmarking (how the results were evaluated): XYZ Med leaders decided they wanted to know several things about their company (obtain information), as well as to evaluate the success of their plan (evaluate information).

Therefore, they used both quantitative and qualitative analysis building off their original benchmark. The training manager performed quantitative analysis at the beginning of the project, at the end of months one and three, and at the end of the project. The qualitative analysis was done at the beginning and end of the project.

Time/duration of project: Three and a half months for project completion, including analysis time and report out—total of four months

Analysis and example:

1. **Quantitative**

    Productivity. Initially, the training manager (TM) went to four of the top-performing individuals in the department and asked them to list the top 10 to 15 activities that they spent their time on.

    From there, the TM asked the VP of the department to deliver a survey to all of the employees in the department, asking them to rank the activities in order of importance to them and to the company and to estimate how much time they spent on them each week. To complete the benchmark, the TM compared the survey results to what the top individuals said they spent time on and to what the employees' managers observed.

    At the end of the time frame, the employees filled out the same survey and the TM compared the numbers to see which areas had increased or decreased.

Talent engagement. At the beginning, the one-month mark, the three-month mark, and the end of the project timeline, employees completed the Talent Engagement Zone assessment. A spike was seen right after the talent training took place (at the one-month mark), but dropped at the three-month point. The TM worked with leaders in the department to spend one-on-one time with the individuals to encourage ongoing support in those areas of strengths and talents.

2. **Qualitative**

For the two qualitative aspects of leadership development and entrepreneurial creativity, sometimes seen as soft-skill assets, the TM decided to focus the interview questions on what mattered most to XYZ Med—in this case, not losing its culture.

The TM could not interview all the people who went through the leadership program that was implemented, so he picked key individuals—managers who did and did not go through the program and employees who worked for those managers. Questions were tailored around the two topics. For those that took the first interview, the second and final interview covered the same questions as the initial interview, with the addition of questions comparing the before and after of the changes in the project.

The TM analyzed the initial interviews at the beginning and the final interview at the end. The differences in trends showed significant improvement in the respect employees felt for their managers who had participated in the program (leadership development) and listed a number of ways they were able to use their own unique voice and talents (such as leading the team, working on new analysis, or creating a different process) to contribute to the company (entrepreneurial creativity).

11.4 Real Stories

Proving the Success of the Program

I had been the leader of two combined departments (see Chapter 1 and Chapter 3 for initial stories) for over six months. It felt like all of these efforts were working, but I had no empirical proof. I wanted to do another engagement survey, but HR said it typically only does the survey once a year for each department, if that, partially for cost reasons and partially because it normally did not see an appreciable change that soon.

I asked the GM if we could have HR do another survey, anyway. One, I was curious if morale and engagement had actually improved. Two, I had an ulterior motive. We were in growth mode, and if the survey results showed significant improvement, I wanted to request additional budget for travel and marketing to increase our activities and results—something each team member intimated they wanted, without exception. I saw an opportunity for a virtuous cycle as it were. Beyond HR, the GM, or even my expectations, we came in at an overall 4.5 (from an original 3.1)! Just as important—or perhaps more importantly—no individual team member's average markings were under a 4.0 in either department! The HR director used words like "unprecedented" and said "I've never seen such improvement over such a relatively short time period."

Needless to say, I was ecstatic to have turned around the low morale, the lack of engagement, and the unhappy and aimless team I inherited to a high-morale, high-performing, engaged and empowered, happy team. I attribute this to having an amazing boss who was understanding and trusting and who gave wide latitude; a concentrated effort on increasing communications—up, down, and sideways; an HR director who was not only good at her job but was also engaged and a partner in effecting change; and the leadership/management lessons I learned from being a US Marine Corps officer.

—Alex Min

Reducing the Time to Fill Open Roles at a Manufacturing Company

A newly appointed VP of HR at a multibillion-dollar company assembled a team of his key HR staff from various locations to reduce the time to fill open jobs, AKA "lead time." He did so because soon after he was hired by the newly appointed turnaround CEO, he heard complaints from his peers about how long it took to fill open positions and about how the manufacturing sites were understaffed and not getting help to fill the roles so they hired external recruiters, which was expensive.

The CEO and the team did some initial data gathering and found:

- More than 300 salaried employees had recently been hired (predominantly in engineering and supply chain).
- Each manufacturing site was responsible for its own recruitment; there was no sharing of candidates between sites/divisions.
- No one tracked lead time or knew the actual recruitment costs.

The team then decided to meet to map the current process and brainstorm how they would get actual data on lead time and costs. The high-level process had seven chunks of work (see Table 11.4) and seemed fairly consistent. The team decided to conduct stakeholder interviews of hiring managers and HR staff as part of the effort.

TABLE 11.4.   Reducing the Time to Fill Open Roles at a Multibillion-Dollar Manufacturing Company

IDENTIFY NEEDS	IDENTIFY SOURCING STRATEGY	ASSESS AND SCREEN	SELECT	PREPARE OFFER	CONDUCT DUE-DILIGENCE	ONBOARD

Current State: 130 days estimated, 160 days actual

Future State: 50 days goal

The group then mapped the detailed process and learned that each location did the process differently. There were 76 hours of work involved in the end-to-end process for five different roles. They estimated the time to be 130 days of total time with the current handoffs and 12 delays, five of which were for approvals, and one of which caused a three-month delay. They identified several wastes including *rework* (e.g., role being redefined during the hiring process or two to three interview visits because of last-minute cancellations by interviewers) and *defects* (e.g., candidate being interviewed who is clearly not qualified, interviewers not being prepared for the interview or asking inappropriate, irrelevant questions).

They had some interesting insights: "we thought we couldn't use social media." They also had been told that the Sarbanes-Oxley Act "required" them to get executive approvals for any job with a salary greater than $80,000. And someone whom they could never identify had told them that start dates should always be on Mondays.

The team thought they could get actual data for lead time and recruiting costs from the sources they used. This included Monster, Indeed, and various recruiters as well as the internal IT system (using the posting dates and actual start dates). After many hours of effort from multiple team members who queried the sources and then called for customer support, they were able to capture data. The actual time to fill the jobs was 160 days (32 weeks). The recruiting cost for external hires was nearly $2 million.

INITIAL—CURRENT STATE PROBLEMS

- Wastes identified: 50
- Pain points identified from surveys: more than 19
- Delays: 12 (one up to three months)
- Steps: 28 (about 80 percent of the steps are done again resulting in additional time)
- Approvals: 5
- Unique templates/forms: more than 20

The group then developed a future-state process that eliminated many of the wastes and customer pain points. The new process embedded an internal recruiting center of excellence that would do most of the candidate qualification and then hand off the remaining work to the hiring manager and local HR staff. The team was excited about their work.

They could see how the new streamlined process would be so much easier and consistent. They felt confident that the hiring managers would be happy to know they could get some internal recruiting help to reduce costs. They left determined to implement the new process in three months.

Four months after the development and implementation of the future-state process, I was in a staff meeting with the division president and his staff. A newly appointed HR person for this division addressed the staff and explained that she could fill the new position on the leadership team within three months.

She explained that the HR team had done some work recently and that she felt confident they would have someone in the role in 8–10 weeks. The leadership team had skeptical looks on their faces. She provided details why she felt confident in the three months: the team had implemented a new process that was much more streamlined with less cost.

COMPLETION—MEASUREMENTS OF SUCCESS

- **Cost Savings:** Nearly $1 million in cost savings (40 percent reduction). Incorporates a center of excellence for recruiting, leveraging sourcing relationships and tapping compensation expertise. Allows local HR to better support the business as a strategic business partner.
- **Delays:** Eliminates approvals (and three-month delays) by establishing decision rules.
- **"Prep Meeting":** Incorporates a planning meeting between hiring manager, HR business partner, and recruiter targeted at identifying best method of sourcing talent, skill sets required, assessment and evaluation approach, interview team, and method for feedback.
- **Standardization:** Standardize forms, templates and process, front-loading steps to prevent loop backs (e.g., hold intake meeting).
- **Collaboration and Efficiency:** Implement a common applicant tracking tool, enabling transparency across all four business units and corporate for all open positions and using "knockout questions."

—Susan Clapham, President, Clapham Consulting

Encouraging Growth—as a Manager

As manager-supervisors, we are or should be committed to developing employees. Along the way we recognize an employee that has developed a skill set comparable to ours and could do our job. Rather than feel threatened by this development as a manager, we should recognize the employee and embrace this as a complement to our team development.

Furthermore, the manager should meet and touch base with the employee to discuss future goals with the developed skill sets and explore how the manager can assist to reach those goals. The manager should give direction and provide opportunities for the employee to experience the supervisory role when that opportunity presents itself, then later meet and discuss the plusses and minuses of the experiences as a teaching moment.

—Rich Sevilla, LP Analyst, Belk

CHAPTER 12

Keeping It Going

12.1 The SBSG Story

It's never good when it's quiet for too long.

It is 3:30 on a Thursday afternoon. Elizabeth is working at her desk, minding her own business, getting work done (and more productively, since she was focusing on her strengths, and not having to do a few things she used to that were not her strengths; she traded those tasks with another person in the TEO shuffle).

Joe pops into her office—so fast and unexpectedly that Elizabeth bangs her knee against the desk. Rubbing her sore knee, she asks, "What's up, boss?"

Joe laughs. "Didn't know I had that surprise factor still in me. OK, so what's next?"

Elizabeth just looks and looks some more. *He couldn't be asking what I think he's asking—we just had the TEO out brief last Friday!* "Next for what?"

"Your next TEO project. You impressed the higher-ups, especially the ones who didn't want to admit that simply giving people what they wanted would allow for higher productivity and perhaps even increase retention. They want more of it. You worked on only a few departments, on a very small scale."

Elizabeth chokes on the coffee she is drinking. Sure, the TEO project was great for business (*I guess?*) but to scale it out to the organization? This is a big step. "Do you think I—we—are ready for this? We just finished—it's so involved and the other projects."

"Don't you have a bit more time on your hands now that you've been through the TEO project?" Joe continues, "What would it look like, Elizabeth? If we rolled the TEO project out to the rest of SBSG? All of the stores, and the rest of the corporate office?"

12.2 The Nuts and Bolts

The last chapter in the book sets out to quickly tie up a few loose ends that will help you close the door on this project *and* set you up for responses, results, and next steps. You may feel a bit of déjà vu as we talk about some of the same topics, such as continuing to get buy-in, but we are doing this intentionally.

Communication is one of the major reasons that organizational change processes break down. The the more that you open the lines of communication for both the previous project and the next one, the more you are set up for continued success as you engage the employee supply chain and optimize employees' overall talent engagement.

Keeping It Going—Getting Buy-In—Again

So, there I was. I had solved some of the most challenging issues facing our team, and most of the people liked the changes. Most of them (overall) were happy with what we'd done. The others were getting there. Life moved on, and we continued on our way—the project was a success.

Or was it? About two months later, a senior manager in another department asked me about the project. She had found out that some of the results of the project (specifically, removing some of the extra steps that her team was doing) impacted her organization. She immediately put a stop to all changes that affected her department—without even trying to understand why the changes were made in the first place.

Oops. The "happily ever after" never happened for me in the end. Eventually, we were able to scrap some of the areas that didn't affect her team, but we did not eliminate the wasted work, and the team begrudgingly went back to doing processes twice, in two different forms.

Moral of the story? Get the word out to cover your bases. In this case, I probably should have talked with other departments that might have considered themselves affected (even if I didn't). In the end, you own it.

Ask the employees in the affected departments for their feedback about the TEO project, and keep them informed about the long-term results. Ask the employees in the affected departments for their feedback about the TEO project, and keep them informed about the long-term results. Send an e-mail (from your boss or the project sponsor if needed!). Host an optional presentation for anyone to attend—and post the slides in a shared location (like the intranet) if available. Ask people:

- What happened?
- What worked?
- What didn't?
- What best practices can be learned?
- Who else should think about doing what you did in your group?
- How can you help them?

In the end, you want the good with the bad—let them know the entire story. One asterisk here: know your culture. Some organizations want more information—in all directions. Others can handle a simple e-mail. Know your audience. And know you'll probably miss one or two of them. Be ready, a little flexible, and keep your good humor!

The next section sheds a light on a few different ways to present the data. Some tactics you may know already. If you don't—see if they would work in your culture. Perhaps it's time to try something new?

Presenting the Data—Your Words Count (and Theirs Do Too)

Presentations have taken a turn in the last decade. They are no longer front and center; they are a backdrop to the key information: you. When you present, think about how you are engaging the audience. Why do they care about the information you are presenting? Let's revisit how people learn through the Learning Pyramid (Figure 12.1).

FIGURE 12.1.   Learning Pyramid

Remember the last time you were taught—I mean, lectured to—in a class? How much of the information do you remember? The lecture format is at the top of this pyramid. You probably retained less than 10 percent of the information and may barely be able to remember the class you took.

On the other end of the pyramid is teaching others. Have you ever been given the chance to present or lead a part of a session? You learn the most that way because you are teaching the information to others.

You may not be able to have your audience teaching others right away, but you can bring them down the pyramid. Can you start the session with some information and then let them discuss the topic—at large or in groups?

PRESENTATION STYLE

If you're delivering a presentation with something like PowerPoint, less is definitely more. One rule of thumb is to have no more than six words per bullet for each bullet point on a slide. The less content you display on each slide, the more your audience will refer to you—the expert—instead of reading the text. Feel free to make yourself notes, but reduce the number of slides and keep the color and format simple. You want your audience to remember the content. You want them to remember *you*.

A few additional suggestions:

- **Key points:** What do you want people to take away? Focus all points around your one to three key takeaways and emphasize them throughout.

- **Images:** Opt for images over text. Again, use no more than six words in each bullet, and try to fit the text on one line.
- **Metaphors and stories:** For technical or abstract concepts, using metaphors and stories engages the audience and makes the content more consumable and relatable.
- **Example:** What is quantitative analysis? It's taking numbers and making sense of them. For example—what is the average number of years people work in your company? Or the expected high or low number of hours to complete a task?
- **Engagement:** Ever suffered through a dull presentation? Yeah, don't make your audience do that. Find a way to make them laugh, engage them with questions, and take breaks. Ask rhetorical questions, or if possible, give them time to answer (and discuss!).

"IF YOU'RE GOING TO PLAY IN TEXAS ... YOU GOTTA HAVE A FIDDLE IN THE BAND"

Yes—this is part of a country song, originally sung by Alabama in 1984. In the song, a band goes to a bar in Texas and begins playing the songs it is known for. However, after a song or two, a cowboy got up and told them that the band was good, but something was missing, and the music wasn't what the audience wanted. They wanted songs the Texas way—with fiddles and a two-step beat. The band obliged and everyone enjoyed the rest of the night.

The same thing applies here. No, I'm not going to ask you to start playing your fiddle literally—but figuratively. Your fiddle is your work, your project, and the results. The people, those whom you are sharing the results with, will recognize the results. However, they may not want to hear the results the way you want to deliver them (via e-mail, or quietly in a newsletter). They want what they want. So, tailor the message to allow everyone to enjoy your "fiddle music" long after you've completed this project.

LET'S TALK ABOUT AN EXAMPLE

If you're from the HR department, some may see you as "we're with the government, we're here to help" or as from the principal's office. (Hate to say it, but I've been there, and I've see it happen.) You're not in their department, so you're not one of their own. What is *their* fiddle work? How do they communicate? Here are a few ideas for connecting:

- **Continuation plan:** Who will run the plan when you're gone? How do they keep the project going after the initial team (yours) is no longer there? See the kaizen chapter (Chapter 10).
- **Get a champion:** Having someone driving once you're gone can be a blessing or a curse. You can make it a blessing if you're able to find someone who bought in early and is still supporting the plan. Bring up this topic in the presentation, and if possible, have the person present part of the results.
- **Keep checking back:** This isn't a full-time job, but remember to touch base. Check in—they'll be surprised, and touching base is a bit like marketing—it keeps the plan fresh in their mind.

Epilogue

You (and the teams you have worked with) have done a lot in 100 days. This time frame is a relatively short one in which to implement change, so you may have only experienced small-scale changes. For the most part, this project should at least have started your team thinking outside the box and going beyond the job description.

However, you have made an impact because you learned what was needed from the people who needed the change, you made an action plan to cover the details, you carried it out, you made sure to bring the right people along, and you finished with proven results.

One hundred days is enough time to make small-scale changes—imagine if this was an ongoing effort with larger-scale changes. You now have the ability to implement a kaizen culture—and continuously improve the team. Your team members could even start leading their own projects.

Just think of the results. Flip through the next few activities and then think about what's next.

You may even need to start at the beginning of the book—because you're ready to do it again. What's next? The impact would be extraordinary!

12.3 Activities and Application

This section will help you think through ways to make your presentation different, informative, and, most importantly, not boring!

How are you going to present the data?

_____

_____

_____

_____

_____

_____

_____

What is the timeline for presenting?

_____

_____

_____

_____

_____

_____

_____

_____

Have you set up a room for the presentation(s)? Sent out the invite? Put the information here:

_____

_____

_____

_____

_____

_____

How do you know the presentation will be effective?

_____

_____

_____

_____

_____

_____

Who will be key players to prepare? These could be people that may not be familiar with the results. You don't want someone to be surprised in the final presentation and have them try to find problems with your work!

_____

_____

_____

_____

_____

_____

Look at the Learning Pyramid in Part 2 of this chapter. What level(s) do you want to use? Why?

_____

_____

_____

_____

_____

_____

_____

_____

Could you use another level below the one you're using (higher up on the retention scale)? Brainstorm—how could you do that?

_____

_____

_____

_____

_____

_____

_____

_____

12.4 Real Stories

Success in a New (and Data-Driven) Environment

Supporting the sales team of a technology company was fun because I had to learn a ton about the technology they sold and serviced. They were the market leader in their region and new competition was forcing them to step up their efforts to retain their current customers and sign on new customers. The engagement involved team wide training, and individual representative support.

Their top IT services representative came to me with a prospect he was struggling with. They agreed to meet him as a courtesy and he had some information that led him to believe they only took the meeting to tell him how happy they were with their current provider. This understandably upset him because he was able to take the preliminary information they provided to craft a deal that would allow him to buy out their existing contract, upgrade their service and equipment, and have them saving money in seven months.

We both knew that forcing this presentation with their current mindset was a mistake and came up with a plan to use their current state of content to our advantage. He started the meeting by asking them what they liked best about their current provider. This caught them by surprise and played right into their plans. When they were done he reinforced the most positive aspects of their answer, quickly demonstrated his understanding of their industry and then asked them several questions about their plans for future scalability, security, and compatibility. His approach was enough to influence their mindset and open the door for his presentation.

At the conclusion of his presentation they asked him if he could come back and give the same presentation to the chief financial officer and the chief information officer. Five months and two meetings later, he secured the technology services contract and opened conversations into potential new equipment contracts.

—Michael Reddington, CFI, Vice President of Executive Education,
Wicklander-Zulawski and Associates

Never Stop Succeeding

As a manager, supervisor, or teacher, your job is always about learning and passing information along to others. Therefore, you will never stop learning, not only from outside sources, but especially from those you teach or lead.

As a leader-teacher, you are only as good as those who support you in your assignment. You may have the overall knowledge of the subject matter, but those who have their hands on the subject daily deal with the issues and ongoing changes and can be the go-to persons as things evolve. Again, the learning process does not just travel down, but a good manager provides the opportunity for the exchange of information to go up and be taught by those who support him. I know from my experiences that some managers feel knowledge is power, so the more they know (learn) and keep to themselves, the more power they have. The manager feels they are necessary (powerful) because they are the go-to person for everyone because they feel they have the knowledge.

The manager feels successful because everything runs smoothly because of the manager's vast knowledge, but this becomes a problem since the manager feels he or she can never be away from the job because nobody else can do the job. Therefore, when the manager is away, nothing appears to work right, because nobody knows how to do things. This is actually a failure of the manager not passing along his or her knowledge for others to learn and use in their absence. We should never stop learning, because knowledge is a powerful tool for everyone to use and share in a working environment to help everyone be successful, not just a few.

First and foremost, my experiences as a teacher at the Newark Unified School District while working as a police officer was some of my most rewarding work. There I learned that knowledge was power to those students, and I learned to pass those experiences along as a field training officer and acting supervisor. I wanted to provide that knowledge to others (students, peers, supervisors, and managers) for their future success and empowerment wherever their life may take them.

Sometimes that reward comes years later when a student becomes a police officer or a peer has success by being promoted through the ranks to chief of police. I recently received an e-mail from that student that said "Thank you, Rich. It is very special getting congratulations from you, as you were always someone that I looked to as a mentor."

—Rich Sevilla, as Officer/Teacher jointly with City of Newark
and Newark Unified School District

The Seven Deadly Sins of Kaizen— the Seven Wastes

Known for many problems, the seven items below (sometimes remembered as "TIMWOOD") should be avoided in all processes in all jobs as much as possible (McBride 2003).

When reading this list, think of your work. These terms apply to both processes in a factory (think, making widgets) and in an office. Challenge yourself to find at least one of each of these wastes in your office. Can you find it? And if so, can you eliminate it?

1. **Transporting.** Can your company more efficiently transport employees and products? Spending half a mile walking to the next meeting is wasted time, and you can't charge your customers for it.
2. **Inventory (unnecessary).** Are you making more than you need to? Do you have piles of work that are waiting for someone else to complete? Those piles are inventory. Try to get rid of them.
3. **Motion (excess).** Do you move back and forth between stations repeatedly? Waste. Not to mention, constant motion like twisting or turning could be a safety or health risk that could lead to injury.
4. **Waiting.** The opposite of inventory is waiting—having nothing in your in-box. Where should the work be coming from? Why don't you have it? Whose signature are you waiting on before you can do your work? How do you reduce time spent waiting?
5. **Overproduction.** Don't know how much product your customer needs? Whether it's creating too many reports internally, or producing too many units externally for the customer external—it doesn't matter. Overproduction is making too much, and therefore you're wasting time and energy (not to mention money!).
6. **Overprocessing.** One way to look at overprocessing is that it's using fancier equipment than needed to do the job. Your customer needs the product in blue, but you deliver 15 different shades of blue. The customer doesn't care about the shade. Simplify the process to what customers really want.

7. **Defections.** This form of waste may be the easiest one of all to describe. You did the work once. Incorrectly. Now you're doing it again—wasting time, money, and energy. Oh, and maybe testing the customer's patience with you if they received the defective product.

Glossary

Action plan—A list of items set in a certain order for the purpose of accomplishing a certain goal or goals.

ADKAR model—Awareness, Desire, Knowledge, Ability, Reinforcement model developed by Jeff Hiatt in 1996 as a framework for preparing, implementing, evaluating, and sustaining change in an organization.

Assessment—Something to measure how much or what a person knows, feels, or believes about a certain topic (Wilbrink 1997).

Attribution error—An incorrect belief of certain influence on an action, person or event. Fundamental attribution error and self-serving bias are in this group.

Bias—A predisposition to see or feel a certain way based on some event or reason.

Conflict—A situation in which your concerns or desires are different from another person's.

Decision bias group—Consisting of escalation of commitment, randomness error, risk aversion, and hindsight bias, a group of mindsets developed in individuals based on their own individual decisions.

Early adopters—People who tend to accept change in a more rapid fashion than most; an example is people who use the latest technology. Within an organization, early adopters are employees who are open to change and are willing to flex to new practices in the organization and could be good resources for influencing the individuals who are not early adopters in their groups or departments.

Emotions—In general, there are believed to be six basic emotions: happiness, anger, fear, sadness, disgust, and surprise.

Employee engagement (EE)—The attitude of a person about a job.

Extrinsic motivation—Motivation that an individual experiences that is external in nature, such as from a manager's verbal appreciation, a promotion, or a raise (the opposite: intrinsic motivation).

Initiative—Taking responsibility for your part of the project, work, or task and making it your job or your focus to make it excellent.

Intervention—An event or series of events to change the current status quo to help or improve the current operation (for example, process, people, culture) to better the company for a certain purpose.

Interview—A method to gather information typically through asking a series of questions.

Intrinsic motivation—Motivation driven internally to an individual, such as for the challenge, the personal reward, or the feeling of completion or accomplishment of the project or task (the opposite: extrinsic motivation).

Kaizen—An event with a focus on process improvement. Originally considered an operations-only focus, it is now used to improve areas from office cubicles to financial budgets to manufacturing. It typically is one to five days in length with a team of four to seven people from different parts of an organization.

Organizational development—Improving an organization, or a part of an organization (such as individual or group) through development using specific techniques to increase an organization's effectiveness (Anderson 2015).

Parking lot—In a brainstorming, problem-solving, or kaizen process-improvement session, it is an area set aside for good ideas that are to be tabled for a later time frame or project.

Perception distortion—A group of biases including selective perception and halo effect. Having this bias can change what you believe you see of others, which could result in a miscommunication, a judgment, or discrimination from what you see versus what another person is actually doing, seeing, or saying.

Politics at work (handling)—Understanding others' viewpoints and managing to those viewpoints (and expectations).

Qualitative data—Data that are delivered through relative terms, such as through interviews or comparisons, using words as a primary source. The data cannot be compared in a specific, numeric way but can be used for trends and other methods for analysis.

Quantitative data—Data that are numerical in nature and can be measured or compared. Examples are a water line before and after a storm, a level-of-productivity increase, or the number of people who obtained a certification, a rating, or a specific level on an assessment.

Raw data—Information, typically numbers or quantitative based, in its original form, such as an output from a survey, an assessment, or an interview. They are typically further analyzed to give ideas for solutions, answers to problems, or strategic direction suggestions.

Red/yellow/green status—A term commonly used in project management as the level of readiness based on planned expectation.

> **Red**—Task is not ready, has a problem, or is behind schedule.

Yellow—Task may not be ready, may have a problem, or is leaning to be behind schedule.

Green—Task is on track, has no expected problems, and is on schedule.

Talent engagement—Maximizing your employees' output to the team, department, or organization by using not only what is required of them but also the talents, skills, and strengths not on the job description.

Talent engagement optimization (TEO)—An action plan to optimize the talent in your company (the employees you already have) and creating a more motivated, efficient, and energized workforce that works around silos and sees beyond the basics of what is required of employees.

References

Introduction

Chat-Uthai, M. 2013. "Leveraging Employee Engagement Surveys Using the Turnover Stimulator Approach: A Case Study of Automotive Enterprises in Thailand." *International Journal of Business and Management* 8, no. 6 (September): 16–21.

Lesko, A. P. 2016a. "Is It Time to Debut Your 'Unseen Picasso'?" Last accessed August 15, 2016. https://www.linkedin.com/pulse/time-debut-your-unseen-picasso-ashley-prisant-lesko-phd.

———. 2016b. "I Didn't Quit My Job, I Fired My Company." October 14, 2016. https://www.linkedin.com/pulse/i-didnt-quit-my-job-fired-company-lessons-leaders-best-lesko-phd/.

Rothwell, N. 2010. *The Engaged University. A Manifesto for Public Engagement.* http://www.campusengage.ie/groups/engaged-universit y-manifesto-public-engagement.

Schaufeli, W. B., and A. B. Bakker. 2003. *Test Manual for the Utrecht Work Engagement Scale.* Unpublished manuscript, Utrecht University, the Netherlands. http://www.schaufeli.com.

Chapter 1

Lencioni, P. 2007. *The Three Signs of a Miserable Job: A Fable for Managers (and Their Employees).* San Francisco, CA: Wiley.

Chapter 2

Anderson. D. L. 2015. *Organization Development: The Process of Leading Organizational Change,* 3rd ed. Thousand Oaks, CA: Sage.

Hiatt, J. 2007. "ADKAR." https://www.prosci.com/adkar.

Sirkin, H. L, P. Keenan, and A. Jackson. 2005. "The Hard Side of Change Management." *Harvard Business Review,* October 2005. https://hbr.org/2005/10/the-hard-side-of-change-management.

Chapter 3

Barnes, M. 2000. "A Theory of Human Motivation." *Classics in the History of Psychology* (online library), August 2000. http://psychclassics.yorku.ca/Maslow/motivation.htm.

Cahill, R. 2006. "What Are Good Questions to Ask Employees in One on One Meetings? I Just Want My Employees to Be Happy and Productive. How Can I Make Sure We're Having Good, Honest, Productive Conversations?" In answer to posted question, Quora, May 26, 2016. https://www.quora.com/What-are-good-questions-to-ask-employees-in-1-1-meetings.

Chat-Uthai, M. 2013. "Leveraging Employee Engagement Surveys Using the Turnover Stimulator Approach: A Case Study of Automotive Enterprises in Thailand." *International Journal of Business and Management* 8, no. 6: 16–21.

Idore, C., and T. Luhby. 2015. "Turns Out Americans Work Really Hard, But Some Want to Work Harder." *CNN Money*, July 9, 2015. http://money.cnn.com/2015/07/09/news/economy/americans-work-bush.

Jones, J. M. 2013. "In U.S., 40% Get Less Than Recommended Amount of Sleep." December 19, 2013, *Gallup News*. http://www.gallup.com/poll/166553/less-recommended-amount-sleep.aspx.

Lesko, A. P. 2015. *New Manager Influences: Probing the Effects of Career Motivation on Work Engagement*. PhD diss., Sullivan University. ProQuest (3729207). https://search.proquest.com/openview/e58ae89686659b75d87f6490f4d77521/1.pdf?pq-origsite=gscholar&cbl=18750&diss=y.

Myers, I. B., M. H. McCaulley, N. L. Quenk, and A. L. Hammer. 2003. *MBTI Manual: A Guide to the Development and Use of the Myers-Briggs Type Indicator*, 3rd ed. Mountain View, CA: CPP Inc.

National Co-ordinating Centre for Public Engagment (NCCPE). 2010. *The Engaged University: A Manifesto for Public Engagement*. http://www.campusengage.ie/sites/default/files/resources/Manifesto%20for%20Public%20Engagement%20Final%20January%202010.pdf.

Schaufeli, W. B., and A. B. Bakker. 2003. *Test Manual for the Utrecht Work Engagement Scale*. Unpublished manuscript, Utrecht University, the Netherlands. http://www.schaufeli.com.

Schein, E. H., and Maanen, J. H. 2013. *Career Anchors: The Changing Nature of Careers Self-Assessment*, 4th ed. San Francisco, CA: Wiley & Sons.

US Navy. 2007. *Division Officer's Personnel Record Form*, NAVPERS 1070/6. http://jcgroove.angelfire.com/DIVO.pdf

Wilbrink, B. 1997. "Assessment in Historical Perspective," *Studies in Educational Evaluation* 23, no. 1 (December): 31–48.

Chapter 4

Bennis, W., and R. J. Thomas. 2002. "Crucibles of Leadership." *Harvard Business Review*, September 2002. https://hbr.org/2002/09/crucibles-of-leadership.

Goman, C. K. 2001. "Seven Seconds to Make a First Impression." *Forbes*, February 13, 2011. https://www.forbes.com/sites/carolkinseygoman/2011/02/13/seven-seconds-to-make-a-first-impression/#55efa57e2722.

Lesko, A. L. 2016a "I Didn't Quit My Job, I Fired My Company: Lessons to Leaders on Saving the Best Assets You Didn't Know You Had." October 14, 2016. https://www.linkedin.com/pulse/i-didnt-quit-my-job-fired-company-lessons-leaders-best-lesko-phd.

Lesko, A. L. 2016b. "Your Coup d'oeil Is Showing." May 17, 2016. https://www.linkedin.com/pulse/your-coup-doeil-showing-ashley-prisant-lesko-phd.

Smith, R., and P. Sawer. 2014. "Inquest Reveals Catalogue of Failures by Heart Surgeon." *Telegraph*, October 26, 2014. http://www.telegraph.co.uk/news/health/news/11187872/Inquest-reveals-catalogue-of-failures-by-heart-surgeon.html.

Chapter 5

Lencioni, P. 2007. "The Three Signs of a Miserable Job." http://www.tablegroup.com/imo/media/doc/Three_Signs_Model.pdf.

Lesko, A. L. 2016. "Do You Know How to Celebrate Your Birthday?" September 15, 2016, https://www.linkedin.com/pulse/do-you-know-how-celebrate-your-birthday-ashley-prisant-lesko-phd.

Musk, E. 2006. "The Secret Tesla Motors Master Plan (Just between You and Me)." *Tesla* (blog), August 2, 2006. https://www.tesla.com/blog/secret-tesla-motors-master-plan-just-between-you-and-me.

National Training Laboratories. n.d. "Learning Pyramid." https://www.fitnyc.edu/files/pdfs/CET_Pyramid.pdf.

Chapter 6

Ashford, S. J., and J. R. Detert. 2015. "Get the Boss to Buy In." *Harvard Business Review*, January–February 2015. https://hbr.org/2015/01/get-the-boss-to-buy-in.

Conner, C. 2013. "Office Politics: Must you Play? A Handbook for Survival/Success." *Forbes*, April 14, 2013. https://www.forbes.com/sites/cherylsnappconner/2013/04/14/office-politics-must-you-play-a-handbook-for-survivalsuccess.

Mochari, I. 2013. "7 Steps for Putting Ideas into Action." *Inc.*, December 28, 2013, http://www.inc.com/ilan-mochari/7-steps-ideas-into-action.html.

Chapter 7

American Management Association. 2004. "Why Projects Fail." http://www.amanet. org/training/articles/Why-Projects-Fail.aspx.

Carlos, T. 2015. "Reasons Why Projects Fail." https://www.projectsmart.co.uk/reasons-why-projects-fail.php.

Geneca. 2011. "Why Up to 75% of Software Projects Will Fail." *Geneca*, March 16, 2011. https://www.geneca.com/blog/software-project-failure-business-development.

International Project Leadership Academy. 2017. "101 Common Causes." http://calleam.com/WTPF/?page_id=2338.

Marr, B. 2016. "Are These the 7 Real Reasons Why Tech Projects Fail? Lack of Accountability." *Forbes*, September 13, 2016. https://www.forbes.com/sites/bernardmarr/2016/09/13/are-these-the-real-reasons-why-tech-projects-fail/#523246ec7320.

Stewart, J. 2015. "Top 10 Reasons Why Projects Fail." November 7, 2015. https://project-management.com/top-10-reasons-why-projects-fail.

Trigg, M. 2015. "The 5 Biggest Reasons Why People Fail: Working with the Wrong People." *Entrepreneur*, May 15, 2015. https://www.entrepreneur.com/article/246279.

West, C. K. 2017. "Four Common Reasons Why Projects Fail." *Project Insight*. http://www.projectinsight.net/white-papers/four-common-reasons-why-projects-fail.

Chapter 8

Anderson, D. L. 2015. *Organizational Development: The Process of Leading Organizational Change*, 3rd ed. Thousand Oaks, CA: Sage.

Reddy, W. B. 1994. *Intervention Skills: Process Consultation for Small Groups and Teams*. San Francisco: Jossey-Bass.

Chapter 9

Burton, N. 2016. "What Are Basic Emotions?" *Psychology Today* (blog). https://www.psychologytoday.com/blog/hide-and-seek/201601/what-are-basic-emotions.

Robbins, S. P., and T. A. Judge. 2014. *Organizational Behavior*, 14th ed. Essex, England: Prentice Hall.

Stein, J. 2017. "Using the Stages of Team Development." *Human Resources at MIT*. http://hrweb.mit.edu/learning-development/learning-topics/teams/articles/stages-development.

Chapter 10

Dictionary.com. "kaizen." http://www.dictionary.com/browse/kaizen.

Vorne. 2017. "Kaizen." http://www.leanproduction.com/kaizen.html.

Additional kaizen reference suggestions:

Dailey, K. W. 2005. *The Kaizen Pocket Handbook*. Port St. Lucie, FL: DW Publishing.

Eckes, G. 2001. *Making Six Sigma Last: Managing the Balance between Cultural and Technical Change*. New York: Wiley.

Mind Tool. n.d. "Kaizen: Gaining the Full Benefits of Continuous Improvement." https://www.mindtools.com/pages/article/newSTR_97.htm.

Chapter 11

Berman, E. 2014. "The Right (and Wrong) Way to Measure Results." *Forbes*, August 19, 2014. https://www.forbes.com/sites/dailymuse/2014/08/19/the-right-and-wrong-way-to-measure-results.

Creswell, J. W. 2012. *Qualitative Inquiry and Research Design: Choosing among Five Approaches*, 3rd ed. Thousand Oaks, CA: Sage.

Chapter 12

National Training Laboratories. n.d. "Learning Pyramid." https://www.fitnyc.edu/files/pdfs/CET_Pyramid.pdf.

Appendix A

McBride, D. M. 2003. "The 7 Wastes in Manufacturing." *EMSS Strategies,* August 29, 2003. http://www.emsstrategies.com/dm090203article2.html.

Glossary

Anderson. D. L. 2015. *Organization Development: The Process of Leading Organizational Change*. 3rd ed. Thousand Oaks, CA: Sage.

Wilbrink, B. 1997. "Assessment in Historical Perspective." *Studies in Educational Evaluation* 23, no. 1 (December): 31–48.

About the Author

Ashley Lesko, SHRM-CP, PhD has a multifaceted background—from working in the military as a Naval Officer and leadership roles in *Fortune* 100 companies, to educating students at colleges and universities and event speaking. A former Surface Warfare Officer, she led hundreds of sailors and employees on ships on both coasts. After receiving her MBA at MIT, she filled various roles at Amazon in Operations, Leadership, and Finance with oversight of more than $45 million and training programs, budgeting, and strategy across multiple fulfillment centers. She now leads Square Peg Solutions, an organization dedicated to helping companies develop leaders through a refined and tested Talent Engagement Optimization process. She also teaches business and HR classes for Harvard Extension and Queens University.

Index